100
LITERACY
FRAMEWORK
LESSONS

IMPNG

Copyrightcholastic
Limited. Al

Save for the may not
be copied,in part or
in any maned use or
activities a

The matered in *100
Literacy Fr*CD-ROM,
or by the tgiven for
purchaserstravenes
Scholastic

This CD-ROthat you
run virus-cept any
responsibiloccur as
a result of

• PC and Mac with a CD-ROM drive and 512 Mb RAM (recommended)
• Windows 98SE or above/Mac OSX.1 or above
• Recommended minimum processor speed: 1 GHz

For all technical support queries, please phone
Scholastic Customer Services on 0845 603 9091

YEAR
4

Scottish Primary

**Sue Graves, Jay Mathews
& Fiona Tomlinson**

CREDITS

Authors
Sue Graves, Jay Mathews
& Fiona Tomlinson

Commissioning Editor
Fiona Tomlinson

Development Editor
Simret Brar

Project Editor
Rachel Mackinnon

Editor
Anne Priestly

Assistant Editor
Roanne Charles

Series Designers
Anna Oliwa &
Joy Monkhouse

Designers
Geraldine Reidy,
Micky Pledge &
Catherine Perera

Book Designer
Q2A Media

Illustrations
Mark Brierly, Andy
Keylock & Peter Lubach /
Beehive Illustration

CD-ROM Development
CD-ROM developed in
association with Vivid
Interactive

Narrative © 2007, Jay Mathews
Non-fiction © 2007, Sue Graves
Poetry © 2007, Fiona Tomlinson
© 2007 Scholastic Ltd

Designed using Adobe InDesign

Published by Scholastic Ltd
Villiers House
Clarendon Avenue
Leamington Spa
Warwickshire CV32 5PR
Visit our website at
www.scholastic.co.uk

Printed by Bell and Bain Ltd
3456789 7890123456

ACKNOWLEDGEMENTS

The publishers gratefully acknowledge permission to reproduce the following copyright material: **Andrew Fusek Peters** for the use of 'Last night I saw the city breathing' from *The moon is on the microphone* by Andrew Fusek Peters © 1997, Andrew Fusek Peters (1997, Sherbourne). **HarperCollins Publishers Ltd** for the use of an extract 'Popular plastic' by Sue Graves from *Trash to treasure* by Sue Graves © 2002, Sue Graves (2002, HarperCollins Publishers Ltd). **Hodder and Stoughton Ltd** for the use of an extract from *Growing up in the forties* edited by Rebecca Hunter © 2001, Hodder Wayland (2001, Hodder Wayland). **Lazy Bee Scripts** for the use of an extract from the playscript *Just like us* by Bill Tordoff © 1990, Lazy Bee Scripts (1990, Lazy Bee Scripts) Full text and performance rights can be obtained from www.lazybeescripts.co.uk **Jay Mathews** for the use of 'The shining pearl – part 1 and 2', 'Facts about Vietnam', 'David loses his cool – part 1 and 2', 'Old Dan and the stray dog – part 1 and 2', 'Letter from Dan Boyd' and 'Dragon land – part 1 and 2' all by Jay Mathews © 2007, Jay Mathews (2007, previously unpublished); for the playscript adaptation 'Granny I'm home!' based on *Bunda's dreamings* by Jay Mathews © 2007, Jay Mathews (2007, previously unpublished); for the extracts 'The lions', 'Thomas and Rosie', and 'Jimmy – part 1 and 2' all from the e-book *Once there were lions* by Roger Hurn © 2005, Jay Mathews (2005, Literacy geos MADD); for the use of text adapted from the audio recount 'Jean's story' from *Once there were lions* CD 3 © 2007, Jay Mathews (Original; 2005, Literacy goes MADD; this extract, 2007, previously unpublished); for the use of 'Simon' adapted from the e-book *Once there were lions* by Roger Hurn © 2005, Jay Mathews; adaptation © 2007, Jay Mathews (Original 2005, Literacy goes MADD; adaptation 2007, previously unpublished); for the use of 'Gran comes to visit – parts 1 and 2' and 'The day the sky was illuminated by a bonfire' both from *Bunda's dreamings* by Jay Mathews © 2006, Jay Mathews (2006, Literacy goes MADD); for the adaptation of 'Gran comes to visit' from *Bunda's dreamings* by Jay Mathews, adaptation © 2007, Jay Mathews; original © 2006, Jay Mathews (adaptation 2007, previously unpublished; original 2006, Literacy goes MADD); for the use of 'The girl – a story from Vietnam – parts 1 and 2' and 'The ghostly woman' both from *East of the sun, west of the moon* by Roger Hurn, illustration by Sue Woollett. Text and illustration © 2005, Jay Mathews (2005, Literacy goes MADD) and for the adaptation of 'Pedro's new friend' by Jay Mathews from 'Pedro's poncho' by Roger Hurn from *East of the sun, west of the moon* by Roger Hurn © 2007, Jay Mathews (original publication 2005, Literacy goes MADD; this version, 2007, previously upublished). **Trevor Millum** for the use of 'Victoria Nicola liked to eat' by Trevor Millum from *Whizz Bang Orang-utan* compiled by John Foster © 1999, Trevor Millum (1999, Oxford University Press). **Judith Nicholls** for the use of 'The Romans in Britain ...A history in 40 words' by Judith Nicholls from *Shadow rap* by Judith Nicholls © 2005, Judith Nicholls (2005, Hodder Murray). **The Peters Fraser and Dunlop Group** for the use of 'A Snow and Ice Poem' by Roger McGough from *Sky in the Pie* by Roger McGough © 1983, Roger McGough (1983, Kestrel Books). **Fiona Tomlinson** for the use of 'Being told off', 'Using my senses' and 'Snowflakes fall softly' all by Fiona Tomlinson © 2007, Fiona Tomlinson (2007, all previously unpublished). **Walker Books Ltd** for the use of extracts from *Benjy's ghost* by Jacqueline Roy © 2004, Jacqueline Roy (2004, Walker Books Ltd); for the use of an extract from *Ignis* by Gina Wilson © 2001, Gina Wilson (2001, Walker Books Ltd) and for the use of text extracts and three illustrations from *When Jessie came across the sea* by Amy Hest and illustrated by P.J. Lynch. Text © 1997, Amy Hest; illustration © 1997, P.J. Lynch (1997, Walker Books Ltd). **Celia Warren** for the use of 'A liking for a Viking' by Celia Warren from *The Works 2* chosen by Brian Moses and Pie Corbett © 2002, Celia Warren (2002, Macmillan Children's Books). **Kit Wright** for the use of 'The magic box' by Kit Wright from *Cat among the pigeons* by Kit Wright © 1987, Kit Wright (1987, Viking Kestrel).

Every effort has been made to trace copyright holders for the works reproduced in this book, and the publishers apologise for any inadvertent omissions.

British Library Cataloguing-in-Publication Data
A catalogue record for this book is available from the British Library.
ISBN 978-0439-94524-0

CONTENTS

INTRODUCTION
100 Literacy Framework Lessons: Year 4

About the series

The *100 Literacy Framework Lessons* series is a response to the Primary National Strategy's revised Literacy Framework and contains **all new** material. The lessons mirror the structure and learning objectives of the Exemplification Units of the Framework. The CD-ROM provides appropriate and exciting texts and also contains a variety of other resources from videos and images to audio and weblinks, which will help to guide you in implementing the Framework's emphasis on ICT texts. The books and CD-ROMs will be an invaluable resource to help you understand and implement the revised Framework.

The key points of the revised framework are:

- The development of early reading and phonics;
- Coherent and progressive teaching of word-level and sentence-level embedded into learning or taught discretely;
- Following and building upon the teaching sequence from reading to writing and developing comprehension;
- Flexible lessons providing a challenging pace;
- Integration of speaking and listening skills;
- Planning for inclusion;
- Broadening and strengthening pedagogy.

Early reading and phonics

The authors of the *100 Literacy Framework Lessons* have endeavoured to incorporate all of the above with one exception, the teaching of phonics. The Government is advising that phonics is taught using a systematic, discrete and time-limited programme. However, where possible we have made links to phonic focuses that you might want to identify when teaching the lesson.

It is important to note that the renewed Framework is advocating a change from the Searchlight model of teaching early reading to the 'simple view of reading', "*The knowledge and skills within the four Searchlight strategies are subsumed within the two dimensions of word recognition and language comprehension of the 'two simple views of reading'. For beginner readers, priority should be given to securing word recognition, knowledge and skills"* (from the PNS Core Papers document). Phonic work will be time limited and as children develop their early reading skills they will then move from learning to read to learning to learn.

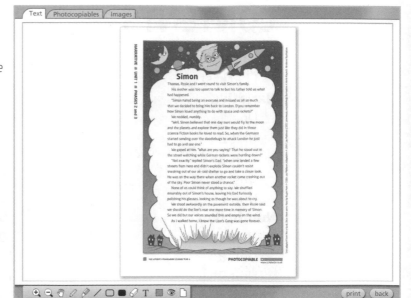

Using the book

The book is divided into three parts, called Blocks: Narrative Block, Non-fiction Block and Poetry Block. This reflects the structure of the renewed Framework planning. The Blocks are divided into Units, each Unit covers a different text-type within the Block, for example in the Narrative Block there might be one Unit which covers 'myths and legends' and another that covers 'plays'. Units are taught on a specified amount of weeks and are split into Phases. Phases vary in length and are essentially a way to focus on a specific part of teaching relating to the Unit. Phases are then divided into days, or lessons, which then contain the teaching activities. Unlike the *100 All New Literacy Hours,* this book has not been divided into terms because one of the main points of the Framework is flexibility and this structure will let teachers adapt to their particular children's needs.

Block [genres] ➤ Units [text-type] ➤ Phases [section of Unit] ➤ Days/Lessons [Individual lessons]

Units

Each Unit covers a different text-type, or genre and because of this each Unit has its own introduction containing the following:

Objectives: All objectives for the Unit are listed under their strand names.

Progression: Statements about the progression that the children should make within the Unit's focus, for example narrative text-type.

Aspects of learning: Key aspects of learning that the Unit covers.

Prior learning: Key elements that the children need to be able to do before they commence the lessons.

Cross-curricular opportunities: Integrating other areas of the curriculum into the literacy lessons.

Resources: Everything required for the lesson that teachers may not have readily available.

Teaching sequence: This is an overview chart of the Unit. It shows the number of Phases, children's objectives, a summary of activities and the learning outcomes.

Unit lesson plans

The lesson plans all follow the same format. There are three columns and each contains different information.

Key features: The key features column provides an at-a-glance view of the key aspects of learning covered in the lesson.

Stages: The stages column provides the main lesson plans.

Additional opportunities: This column provides additional opportunities for the lesson. This is where there will be links made to phonics, high frequency words, support or extension activities and any other relevant learning opportunities.

End of Phase

At the end of each Phase there are three boxes containing Guided reading or writing ideas, Assessment ideas and Further work.

Guided: The guided box contains ideas for guided reading or writing. These have been included separately as there seems to be a trend to do this work outside of the literacy hour lesson. These ideas can either be integrated into a lesson or taught at a separate time.

Assessment: There are two types of assessment.

End of Phase assessments: These are mainly observations of the children or simple tasks to see whether they have understood what has been taught in the Phase. Teachers are referred back to the learning outcomes in the teaching sequence in the Unit introduction.

End of Unit assessments: These are activities which range from interactive activities, to working from a stimulus image, to completing a photocopiable sheet. They can be found on the CD-ROM accompanying this series.

Further work: Further work provides opportunities for the teacher to extend or support the children following the assessment activity.

Photocopiable pages

At the end of each Unit are the photocopiable pages. These can also be found on the CD-ROM.

Using the CD-ROM

This is a basic guide for using the CD-ROM; for more detailed information please go to 'How to use the CD-ROM' on the start-up screen of the CD-ROM.

The CD-ROM contains resources for each book in the series. These might include: text extracts, differentiated text extracts, editable text extracts, photocopiable pages, interactive activities, images, videos, audio files, PowerPoint files, weblinks and assessment activities. There are also skeleton frames based on Sue Palmer's skeletons for teaching non-fiction text types. Also on the CD-ROM are the lesson notes for easy planning as Word file documents.

You can access resources in a number of ways:

Phase menu: The Phase menu provides all the resources used in that Phase. There are tabs at the top of the page denoting the resource type, for example 'Text'. If you click on this tab you will see a series of buttons to your left; if you press these then you will be taken to the other texts used within that Phase. You can print two versions of the text: either the screen – which shows any annotations made (see Whiteboard tools below) or Print PDF version, which will print an A4 size.

Resources menu: The resource menu lists every resource that is available on the CD-ROM. You can search by type of resource.

Whiteboard tools: This series contains a set of whiteboard tools. These can be used with any interactive whiteboard and from a computer connected to a projector. The tools available are: Hand tool – so that when you zoom in you can move around the screen; Zoom in; Zoom out; Pen tool for freehand writing or drawing; Highlighter; Line tool; Box tool; Text tool; Eraser tool; Clear screen; Hide annotations; Colour. You cannot save any changes made to the texts so always remember to 'Print Screen' when you annotate the CD-ROM pages.

Children in gas masks

Speak and listen for a range of purposes on paper and on screen strand checklist

	Narrative Unit 1	Narrative Unit 2	Narrative Unit 3	Narrative Unit 4	Narrative Unit 5	Non-fiction Unit 1	Non-fiction Unit 2	Non-fiction Unit 3	Non-fiction Unit 4	Poetry Unit 1	Poetry Unit 2
Strand 1 Speaking											
Offer reasons and evidence for their views, considering differing opinions.											
Respond appropriately to the contributions of others in light of differing viewpoints.								✔	✔	✔	✔
Tell stories effectively and convey detailed information coherently for listeners.	✔	✔				✔	✔				
Use and reflect on some ground rules for sustaining talk and interaction.			✔		✔						
Strand 2 Listening and responding											
Listen to a speaker, make notes on the talk and use notes to develop a role play.							✔				
Compare the different contributions of music, words and images in short extracts from TV programmes.	✔		✔			✔			✔		
Identify how talk varies with age, familiarity, gender and purpose.			✔					✔	✔		
Strand 3 Group discussion and interaction											
Take different roles in groups and use the language appropriate to them, including roles of leader, reportr, scribe and mentor.							✔				
Use time, resources and group members efficiently by distributing tasks, checking progress, making back-up plans.											
Identify the main points of each speaker, compare their arguments and how they are presented.											
Strand 4 Drama											
Create roles showing how behaviour can be interpreted from different viewpoints.			✔	✔	✔	✔	✔				
Develop scripts based on improvisation.					✔						
Comment constructively on plays and performances, discussing effects and how they are achieved.					✔						

Read for a range of purposes on paper and on screen strand checklist

	Narrative Unit 1	Narrative Unit 2	Narrative Unit 3	Narrative Unit 4	Narrative Unit 5	Non-fiction Unit 1	Non-fiction Unit 2	Non-fiction Unit 3	Non-fiction Unit 4	Poetry Unit 1	Poetry Unit 2
Strand 5 Word recognition											
Objectives covered by the end of Year 2.											
Strand 6 Word structure and spelling											
Use knowledge of phonics, morphology and etymology to spell new and unfamiliar words.										✔	
Distinguish the spelling and meaning of common homophones.											
Know and apply common rules.											
Develop a range of personal strategies for learning new and irregular words.											
Strand 7 Understanding and interpreting texts											
Identify and summarise evidence from a text to support a hypothesis.			✔			✔					
Deduce characters' reasons for behaviour from their actions and explain how ideas are developed in non-fiction texts.	✔		✔	✔	✔		✔	✔			
Use knowledge of different organisational features of texts to find information effectively.								✔			
Use knowledge of word structures and origins to develop their understanding of word meanings.											
Explain how writers use figurative and expressive language to create images and atmosphere.		✔	✔	✔	✔				✔	✔	✔
Strand 8 Engaging with and responding to texts											
Read extensively favourite authors/genres and experiment with other types of text.		✔	✔				✔	✔		✔	✔
Interrogate texts to deepen and clarify understanding and response.	✔		✔			✔	✔	✔	✔	✔	✔
Explore why and how writers write, including through face-to-face and online contact with authors.			✔							✔	✔

Write for a range of purposes on paper and on screen strand checklist

	Narrative Unit 1	Narrative Unit 2	Narrative Unit 3	Narrative Unit 4	Narrative Unit 5	Non-fiction Unit 1	Non-fiction Unit 2	Non-fiction Unit 3	Non-fiction Unit 4	Poetry Unit 1	Poetry Unit 2
Strand 9 Creating and shaping texts											
Develop and refine ideas in writing using planning and problem-solving strategies.	✔	✔	✔	✔	✔	✔	✔	✔	✔	✔	
Use settings and characterisation to engage readers' interest.	✔	✔		✔							
Summarise and shape material and ideas from different sources to write convincing and informative non-narrative texts.						✔	✔	✔			
Show imagination through language used to create emphasis, humour, atmosphere or suspense.		✔	✔	✔	✔				✔		
Choose and combine words, images and other features for particular effects.			✔	✔	✔	✔	✔		✔	✔	✔
Strand 10 Text structure and organisation											
Organise texts into paragraphs to distinguish between different information, events or processes.	✔	✔	✔	✔		✔	✔	✔			
Use adverbs and conjunctions to establish cohesion within paragraphs.		✔				✔	✔				
Strand 11 Sentence structure and punctuation											
Clarify meaning and point of view by using varied sentence structure (phrases, clauses and adverbials).		✔		✔	✔		✔	✔	✔		
Use commas to mark clauses and the apostrophe for possession.			✔	✔			✔	✔			
Strand 12 Presentation											
Write consistently with neat legible and joined handwriting.	✔	✔			✔					✔	✔
Use word-processing packages to present written work and continue to increase speed and accuracy in typing.						✔		✔	✔		✔

NARRATIVE
UNIT 1 Stories with historical settings

Speak and listen for a range of purposes on paper and on screen

Strand 1 Speaking
- Tell stories effectively and convey detailed information coherently for listeners.

Strand 2 Listening and responding
- Compare the different contributions of music, words and images in short extracts from TV programmes.

Read for a range of purposes on paper and on screen

Strand 7 Understanding and interpreting texts
- Deduce characters' reasons for behaviour from their actions and explain how ideas are developed in non-fiction texts.

Strand 8 Engaging with and responding to texts
- Interrogate texts to deepen and clarify understanding and response.

Write for a range of purposes on paper and on screen

Strand 9 Creating and shaping texts
- Develop and refine ideas in writing using planning and problem-solving strategies.
- Use settings and characterisation to engage readers' interest.

Strand 10 Text structure and organisation
- Organise texts into paragraphs to distinguish between different information, events or processes.

Strand 12 Presentation
- Use word-processing packages to present written work and continue to increase speed and accuracy in typing.

Progression in narrative

In this year children are moving towards:
- Recognising the stages in a story and identifying the introduction, build-up, climax or conflict and resolution; noticing how the passing of time is conveyed and key words and phrases used to introduce paragraphs or chapters; identifying the events that are presented in more detail and those that are skimmed over.
- Expressing response to particular characters and identifying techniques used by the author to persuade the reader to feel sympathy or dislike.
- Recognising the way that the historical setting affects characters' appearance, actions and relationships; commenting on differences between what characters say and what they do. Making deductions about the feelings and motives that might lie behind their words.
- Looking at the way that a historical setting is created using small details and longer descriptions; noting similarities and differences with their own experiences.
- Planning, telling and writing short stories set in the past; including descriptive details to evoke the historical setting and make it more vivid; sequencing events clearly and show how one event leads to another; using a range of connectives to show changes in time and place.

▶

UNIT 1 ◄ Stories with historical settings continued

Key aspects of learning covered in this Unit

Creative thinking
Children will be encouraged to use their historical knowledge and their imaginations to create a setting and a new story set in the past.

Empathy
Exploring historical settings and events through narrative will help children to develop a sense of empathy with historical characters and an understanding of their way of life.

Self-awareness
Children will discuss and reflect on their personal responses to the texts.

Communication
Children will often work collaboratively in pairs and groups. They will communicate outcomes orally, in writing and using other modes and media where appropriate.

Prior learning

Before starting this Unit check that the children can:
■ Recognise typical characters, settings and events in adventure stories.
■ Write an adventure story that has: a problem and a resolution; paragraphs and/or chapters with connectives to signal time, sequence or place; descriptions of typical setting and characters; written dialogue that moves the plot on.
■ Tell a story for an audience with events in sequence, change voice for different characters and include story language.
If they need further support please refer to a prior Unit or a similar Unit in Year 3.

Resources

Phase 1:
Jean's story by Jean Pearce �; *The lions, Thomas and Rosie, Jimmy parts 1* and *2* by Roger Hurn ✻; DVD or video of Goodnight Mister Tom (copyright permitting); Soft toy or circle time prop, musical instruments, prop box for Tom and William (optional – see Day 6); Photocopiable page 22 'Features of historical stories'; Photocopiable page 23 'Characterisation chart'; Photocopiable page 24 'Facts, inferences and feelings'; *Rosie's diary* by Jay Mathews ✻; Another story set during the Second World War

Phase 2:
Simon by Roger Hurn ✻; Circle time object; *The Diary of a Young Girl* by Anne Frank; *David loses his cool parts 1* and *2* by Jay Mathews ✻; Photocopiable page 25 'Story mountain'; *Once There Were Lions* by Roger Hurn; Another story set in the 1940s

Phase 3:
Photograph of 1941 family ✻; Circle time toy; Story props appropriate to the photograph (optional); *Simon* by Roger Hurn ✻; Word-processing and graphics software; Photocopiable page 25 'Story mountain'; Photocopiable page 26 'Into the picture'; Further historical stories; Assessment activity 'Historical story' ✻

Cross-curricular opportunities

History topic about Second World War
SEAL activities dealing with loss, fear, friendship, growing up

UNIT 1 ■ Teaching sequence

Phase	Children's objectives	Summary of activities	Learning outcomes
1	I can find clues in a story which tell me when the story takes place. I can compare two stories set in the same period of time. I can describe how different characters are feeling in stories by finding clues within the text. I can find information about main characters in stories and understand how the author uses descriptive words and phrases to help the reader like or dislike them. I can write a character sketch on a character from a story. I understand that music, sound effects and costumes help bring a story alive in TV, plays or films.	Look at the way that a historical setting is created using small details and longer descriptions. Note similarities and differences with children's own experiences. Express responses to particular characters and identify techniques used by the author to persuade the reader to feel sympathy or dislike. Analyse how an author makes us feel a certain way about different characters. Build up character profiles. Explore interesting vocabulary. Think about how films, TV and plays can add other dimensions and textures to a story.	Children can read stories with a historical setting and find evidence about the period when the story is set.
2	I can plan a story using the structure of 'beginning, build-up, climax, resolution'. I understand why authors pay more attention to some aspects of a story and give the reader more detail in others. I can identify powerful verbs and connectives in stories.	Plan a simple story using story skeletons/story mountains. Look at ways authors skim some details but expand on others. Use powerful verbs.	Children can recognise the stages in a story and the way that events are linked; identify powerful verbs in a text and talk about their function.
3	I can find clues in a photograph about the period of history in which it was taken. I can discuss who might live and work in the place where a photograph was taken. I can plan a historical story. I can tell a story. I can write an effective start to a story. I know that there can be a difference between what characters say in stories and what they are feeling and thinking.	Analyse characters in a 1940s photograph. Explore what is happening in the setting and how this impacts on the main characters. Plan a short story set in the past including descriptive detail to evoke the historical setting and make it more vivid. Tell an effective story using paragraphs, powerful verbs and connectives. Write an exciting story beginning using vivid descriptions, powerful verbs and connectives. Comment on the difference between what characters say and what they do. Write a historical story.	Children can plan, tell and write stories set in the past. They include detail to evoke the historical setting; sequence events clearly and show how one event leads to another.

Provide copies of the objectives for the children.

DAY 1 ◼ History detectives

Key features	Stages	Additional opportunities
Empathy: explore historical settings and events through narrative **Communication:** work collaboratively in pairs	**Introduction** Tell the children you are going to read them a true story. Don't give them any clues about the content or the time in history in which the story is set. Read the children the true account of *Jean's story* from the CD-ROM. **Speaking and listening** Lead a discussion to find out the facts which the class can recall about the Second World War. Invite the class to hot-seat you as a child from the 1940s and ask you questions about what life was like for children during the blitz in cities. **Independent work** Organise the class into pairs. Give each pair a copy of *Jean's story*. Invite them to read the account again and be 'history detectives' – searching for clues about the time the account takes place: now, in the past, in the future? Now ask them to find more clues in the text which indicate the time in history that the account is set. Give each pair a highlighter pen and ask them to highlight relevant parts of the text. Ask the pairs to decide on roles for this activity – one to be scribe, the other to be reporter. **Plenary** Ask the pairs to report back to the class about their findings. Encourage the listeners to ask questions and to comment on each other's presentations. Gather their ideas together on the board.	**Extend:** find some of the MFW for Year 4 in the texts

DAY 2 ◼ Small details

Key features	Stages	Additional opportunities
	Introduction Have any of the children ever had a special place (den) where the go to meet their friends or just to hide away from everyone for a while? Ask a few volunteers to describe their 'dens.' Read the class *The lions* from the CD-ROM, taken from chapter 1 of *Once There Were Lions.* Draw the children's attention to the way the author makes use of small details to create a clear picture in the reader's mind of the people and places described.	
Empathy: explore historical settings and events	**Speaking and listening** Ask the children to discuss in pairs the two stories already read. They are stories from the same period. Look for the features of historical settings such as: a distinctive setting, fictional characters based on historical details. Can the children find any similarities between the two stories? Encourage them to compare clues about life for children in the 1940s and now. What are the similarities and what are the differences? Are there any issues about life in the Second World War as described in the stories, which are different from the lifestyles of children now?	**Support:** support pairs with reading and scribing
	Independent work Give pairs of children copies of photocopiable page 22 'Features of historical stories' and challenge them to complete the chart with facts and inferences from the two texts.	**Extend:** research other stories written about the Second World War or set in the 1930s/1940s
	Plenary Encourage each pair to share their findings with the class.	

DAY 3 ▮ Vivid descriptions

Key features	Stages	Additional opportunities
Empathy: recognise and label the feelings of others	### Introduction Read *Thomas and Rosie* from the CD-ROM, taken from chapter 2 of *Once There Were Lions*. Can the children describe how different characters were feeling at certain points in the story? For example: Mum when she is saying goodbye to Rosie and Thomas, Thomas when the train started to leave Waterloo station, the girl who wasn't picked by anyone. How would the class feel in the same situation? Discuss how, by using certain descriptive language, the author has made the writing much stronger.	
Communication: work collaboratively	### Independent work Organise groups of four. Each group should have a narrator, two actors and a director. Invite each group to role play a short scenario from the text. ### Speaking and listening Each group should organise a short scene, narrated by the storyteller and acted by the actors. Encourage the narrators to use exciting and interesting vocabulary in their storytelling. Encourage the groups to use the illustrations to help them create a frozen picture (freeze-frame) to start their scenes, which come alive as the narrator tells the story. ### Plenary Ask some groups to perform their scenes. Invite the 'audience' to comment on the use of exciting and interesting vocabulary by the storyteller and the effective body language and facial expressions of the actors.	**Support:** sketch a moment in time from their role play and annotate it with exciting vocabulary **Extend:** write their group's story in the form of a story-strip, illustrate and add thought bubbles

DAY 4 ▮ Characterisation

Key features	Stages	Additional opportunities
	### Introduction In pairs, A and B. 'A' talks to 'B' for one minute about themselves – strengths, personality, likes and dislikes. 'B' then reports to the class one interesting and important point from 'A's' talk then adds something positive about 'A' from his/her own perspective: *Jane is always kind to me when I feel upset; James has a really good singing voice.*	
Self-awareness: discuss and reflect on personal responses **Empathy:** explore historical settings to gain an understanding of characters	### Independent work Explain that in this session the children are going to gather some information from a text about two main characters from, *Once There Were Lions*. Give each pair of children copies of the two extracts, *Jimmy* from the CD-ROM. Read them through. Ask them to discuss in pairs what they thought of the story – Did they like it? Why? Which characters did they like and which did they dislike? Why? Ask some pairs to search the text for facts about Jimmy and some inferences they can make using the text and illustrations. Invite other pairs to collect facts and make inferences about Raymond. Give each child a copy of photocopiable page 23 'Characterisation chart'. Ask them to complete each row of the chart with a different fact from the text about their character.	**Support:** create an *Acknowledgement wall* and invite the children to write supportive and positive comments about their friends and peers on sticky notes and then stick them onto the wall
	### Plenary Read part of a favourite story and ask the children to identify characters they like and those they don't like. Ask them to use references from the text to support their responses.	

DAY 5 ▪ Character sketches

Key features	Stages	Additional opportunities
	Introduction Revisit the two extracts *Jimmy* from the CD-ROM with the children. Ask each pair to devise a question they would like to ask Jimmy or Raymond if they could meet them. You (or a confident child) sit on the hot-seat and answer their questions as either Jimmy or Raymond!	
	Speaking and listening Sit the class in a circle and pass a soft toy around. Each child in turn says something they now know or feel about Jimmy from exploring his character. They should be able to understand more about the way he is feeling, so you can ask: *Do you think Jimmy is hiding anything? Do his actions demonstrate the same thing as his words?* For example: When Jimmy is winding Raymond up, he sounds really aggressive but we know from hot-seating that he is really scared and feels he has to carry on because the other children are cheering him on. Repeat the circle task with information about Raymond.	
Empathy: understand the perspective of another person	**Independent work** Now the children know more about the main characters ask them to write a character sketch about either Jimmy or Raymond under the paragraph headings *Facts, Inferences, Feelings.* Give them photocopiable page 24 'Facts, inferences and feelings', which encourages them to include facts from the story and the hot-seating activity plus 'between the lines' inferences.	**Character development:** describe how Jimmy might react in other situations
	Plenary Listen to some of the character sketches together and encourage comments.	

DAY 6 ▪ Dramatic effects

Key features	Stages	Additional opportunities
Self-awareness: express own views, opinions and preferences	**Introduction** Play a sequence of the television drama, *Goodnight Mister Tom* (copyright permitting). Use the part where William is 'dumped' on Tom by the billeting officer and is invited by Tom into his home for the first time. Can the children tell you what time in history the drama is set? What evidence is there in the sequence? Show the clip again, and this time look for features that paper-based stories do not have, such as: sound effects and music, costume, real setting. Ask for opinions about the impact these have on the dramatic effects of the scene. Demonstrate the impact music has in films and plays, for example giving clues about the emotions of the characters, or a warning about what is about to happen! Ask a child to read a passage from a favourite book which evokes a certain atmosphere (eerie, happy, sad). Invite some others to create the atmosphere with background sounds, such as a cheerful song or a low discordant, tense sound. What does this do for the listener?	**Support:** draw a picture of William while he is sitting in the graveyard looking up at the angel tombstone; draw some speech or thought bubbles and write ideas of his thoughts and speech
Creative thinking: use imagination to create a role **Communication:** work collaboratively to perform a role play	**Speaking and listening** In small groups, ask the children to recreate the action in the clip. If possible, provide a 'prop box' of items to help them get into role. The groups should create their own sound effects or music to help build the drama of the action, using percussion instruments or 'found sounds', voice and 'body percussion'. **Plenary** Invite some groups to perform their role plays. What does the audience think of them? Do the props and the music enhance or detract from the action?	**Extend:** draw a 'graphic score' to record the musical score to accompany the action

Guided reading

Explain that the group are going to read an extract from *Rosie's diary* independently (print this out from the CD-ROM).

Encourage them to use familiar strategies for predicting the meaning of unfamiliar words (context, reading on).

Ask the children what facts they discovered from the text that give clear clues about the time in history in which the story is set.

Assessment

Read the children an extract from another story based in the same period of history. Ask the class:
Where does this story take place?
What evidence is there to prove this?
Observe the children's role plays and group work, focusing on their use of language and empathy with the period and characters.
Refer back to the learning outcomes on page 11.

Further work

Invite pairs of children to research some facts about children in the Second World War. They could give short slideshow presentations to the class.

Now ask the class to revisit the story used in the assessment to look again for more clues about the period in history.

DAY 1 ■ Story mountains

Key features	Stages	Additional opportunities
Self-awareness: discuss and reflect on their personal responses to the texts	**Introduction** Read the extract *Simon* from the CD-ROM. Invite the children to offer their thoughts and feelings. Display photocopiable page 25 'Story mountain'. Discuss the structure of the story and invite the children to suggest where each part fits onto the different parts of the story mountain. For example: Beginning – *Simon hated being an evacuee...* Build up – *Simon's dad said that Simon was fascinated by rockets...* Climax – *He was on his way there when...* Resolution – *Poor old Simon never stood a chance...* Give the children another extract from the story and challenge them, in pairs, to identify the stages.	
Creative thinking: use historical knowledge and imagination to create a new story	**Speaking and listening** Organise the class into small groups. Challenge them to role play a simple story, such as *A night in the air raid shelter*. Encourage them to plan their role plays using the same story mountain structure – beginning, build-up, climax, resolution. Invite a few groups to perform their role plays.	**Support:** act as a scribe and encourage children to create a story using the story mountain as a guide
	Independent work Give each child the photocopiable sheet and ask them to complete the planning of their role play as if they are going to record it as a story.	**Extend:** write their own collection of short stories to create their own book
Communication: work collaboratively	**Plenary** Sit in a circle. Challenge the children to develop a class historical story. Pass an object around. Each child adds a small part to the story. Keep the story mountain framework in mind.	

DAY 2 ■ Timelines

Key features	Stages	Additional opportunities
Empathy: explore a narrative to develop understanding of historical characters	**Introduction** Ask the children if any of them keep diaries. Talk about the reasons why people keep diaries. Do the children know about another diary kept by Anne Frank during the Second World War? Why is it famous? Read *Rosie's diary* from the CD-ROM, with the class. Focus on the episodes in *Rosie's diary* which are dealt with briefly and which take longer to describe. Encourage the children to speculate why this is, perhaps the writer places more importance on one episode, glossing over other episodes because they are painful, or less interesting. Discuss that diaries log the passing of time for posterity.	**Support:** children record their actions for one day; ask them to focus on one which is more important than the others and draw a picture of the event then write about it
	Speaking and listening Organise the class into pairs. Invite one child in each pair to talk their partner through their morning routine of things they did before coming to school. Draw a simple timeline on the board. Ask a volunteer to describe their routine as you write each significant stage onto the time line.	**Extend:** give a group a copy of the diary of Anne Frank and ask them to identify some events on which Anne has focused and why
Communication: work collaboratively	**Independent work** Give each pair a piece of paper and a pen and ask them to create a timeline showing one of the pair's morning routine. Ask the question – *If you were writing this, which episodes would you focus on as being more significant?*	
	Plenary Choose one child's timeline and create a freeze-frame timeline in the classroom using the children in groups to create a series of tableaux.	

DAY 3 ▪ Powerful verbs

Key features	Stages	Additional opportunities
	## Introduction	
	Ask the children to *walk* (action verb) around the classroom or hall, following their own pathways. On command, *freeze*, they stand still and listen for your instruction. Give them another action verb *run, hop, crawl*.	**Support:** role play the text, discuss how the actors can demonstrate the emotions through their body language and facial expressions
	Gather the class together and discuss action verbs. Take each action verb and try to think of another one which is more exciting, interesting or emotive for example: *run – scurry, canter, gallop, pound; hop – spring, leap, vault; crawl – slither, edge, wriggle*. (The children might enjoy looking in a thesaurus for some other ideas.) Repeat the action verb journey but this time use the new powerful verbs. Ask half the class to watch the other half and then comment on the way the movements become more specific and dramatic when the verb is powerful.	
Self-awareness: discuss and reflect on personal responses to a text	## Independent work	**Extend:** a small group develop a 'what happened next' scenario about David and role play it with narration
	Read an extract from *Once There Were Lions*. In pairs, can the children: Pick out the powerful verbs – words that make the sentences strong such as, *bombarded, puffing, pounded, unleashed* and identify the way events are linked – *the next moment, later on, anyway, after that?* Read them *David loses his cool parts 1* and *2* from the CD-ROM. It is a description of a boy in 1940 who is in a very angry mood because he is being evacuated and doesn't want to leave his home and family. Ask the children to discuss their feelings about the story, including how the events are linked, how powerful verbs help create the atmosphere. Give each child a copy of the piece of text with verbs and connectives missing. Challenge them to incorporate their own ideas.	
Communication: share outcomes with the class	## Plenary	
	Share the children's verbs and connectives as a class.	

Guided reading and writing

Ask the children, in pairs, to choose a chapter from *Once There Were Lions* and read it together.
Give them a copy of photocopiable page 25 'Story mountain' and ask them to plot their chapter on the story mountain, as beginning, build-up, climax, resolution.

Assessment

Read a chapter from a story set in the 1940s. Ask pairs to note evidence that the story is set in the past. Share their evidence as a group. One member of the group collates the information on the flipchart.
Discuss whether the children think this is a good book and why they have formed these opinions.
Read the chapter together as a group. Discuss the following: what feelings the writing evokes; the part 'powerful verbs' play in the writing; how the author connects each part of the story (connectives).
Refer back to the learning outcomes on page 11.

Further work

Stand the children in a circle. Place flash cards containing powerful verbs in the centre.
Start a story circle – one child after another telling a part of the story. The challenge is to use verbs from the centre of the circle. When one is used it is turned over and cannot be used again.

DAY 1 ▪ Into the picture

Key features	Stages	Additional opportunities
	### Introduction Ask the children in groups of two or three to imagine they are just about to have their photograph taken. They should discuss the setting (where they are), the people (who they are) and the occasion (what they are doing). Over the next few days, the children are going to gather information, experiences, facts and feelings together to bring to a historical story of their own. Display the image from the CD-ROM of the girl her mother and brother walking along Blackheath High Street in 1941.	
Empathy: explore historical settings to develop an understanding of characters	### Independent work Let the groups discuss what they can see in the picture. What clues are there about the period of history? Looking at the expressions on the faces of the three main characters, what do the children think they are feeling or thinking? Where have they come from? Where are they going? Give groups copies of photocopiable page 26 'Into the picture' and ask them to fill the boxes with their own thoughts and ideas.	**Support:** draw a picture of one of the characters in the photograph and write some words and phrases about what the character is thinking and feeling
Creative thinking: use their historical knowledge and their imagination to create a setting and a new story set in the past	### Speaking and listening In threes, freeze-frame the picture (one child as mum, one as the girl, one as the boy). Bring the freeze-frames alive. What are the characters thinking and saying? Then ask the groups to develop a role play which shows the characteristics of each person, their thoughts, feelings, personality. ### Plenary View a few scenes and discuss the characterisations and storyline developed. Make a list of ideas under the headings *Setting*, *Character* and *Event*.	**Extend:** provide historical stories and ask children to analyse one of the main characters

DAY 2 ▪ In the background

Key features	Stages	Additional opportunities
	### Introduction Look again at the photograph of the family. What can the children see in the background? In pairs, ask them to discuss the picture. Who might live and work in the setting? Write their ideas on the board.	
Empathy: explore historical settings and events through narrative to develop a sense of empathy with historical characters and an understanding of their way of life	### Speaking and listening Put the class into groups of three or four and ask them to pick some of the town people on the list and bring the town street alive starting and ending with a freeze-frame. Discuss with each group what relationship their characters might have with each other. Write their ideas on the board. Ask the children to think about what their character would be talking about – general chat about the war, rationing, blackouts and so on. Encourage each character to have one line to say only and to decide on an order for saying them to avoid everyone speaking at once. Bring the class back together, watch some of the town scenes and invite the audience to comment on highlights. Write their ideas on the board.	**Support:** work with a group to help them to develop their role play **Extend:** create a playscript from their improvised role-play scenes
	### Independent work Ask the children to write their characters' 'one liners' onto big cut out speech bubbles and stick them onto a 'town speech' chart. ### Plenary Organise the class into pairs to introduce their characters to each other.	

DAY 3 ■ Story planning

Key features	Stages	Additional opportunities
Creative thinking: create a setting and a new story set in the past	**Introduction** Explain to the children that together you are going to plan a story about the characters in the photograph. Firstly you need to invent a good story title. As an example of how to choose a title, suggest *Once There Were Lions. Why did the author choose this title?* (The name of the children's den, the fact that they are meeting at the end of the war – more grown up and worldly wise.) **Speaking and listening** Put the children into pairs (where possible mix girls and boys). Ask them to write a title for a story about the characters in the picture. Tell them to brainstorm using all their senses and note descriptive words and phrases, events that might have happened just before the photograph was taken (perhaps the father was injured in a bombing incident) and what might happen after the photograph was taken, (they rush to the hospital to see him). **Independent work** Give the children, in pairs, a copy of the photograph plus photocopiable page 25 'Story mountain'. Ask them to plan a story based on one of the characters in the photograph, the title for the story they invented and including their ideas for what happened before and after the photograph. Encourage them to use historical facts in their story to give it a sense of time. **Plenary** Share some of the planning as a class. Is there evidence of clear structure, including a build-up, climax and resolution?	**Support:** some children might need some extra support, so share a series of story titles with them and discuss reasons why they think the author used that particular title **Extend:** some children could add more characters to their story and make them interact in such a way as to show the relationship and their personalities

DAY 4 ■ Storytelling

Key features	Stages	Additional opportunities
Communication: work collaboratively in pairs and groups; communicate outcomes orally, in writing and using other modes and media where appropriate	**Introduction** Pull together all the threads from the previous three lessons: photograph as a starting point for a story; people who work or live in the setting, the main characters, what happened before and after the photograph was taken; historical names and facts; ideas for story plots. **Speaking and listening** Organise a circle story. Pass a toy around the circle and ask each child to tell the next part of the story about the three main characters from the photograph used in previous lessons. Ask three children to come into the centre of the circle and mime/act the class story as it develops. **Independent work** In pairs, the children are going to tell their own story using their story planning from Day 2. Remind them about making links between events (connectives), vivid descriptions and powerful verbs. The children should bring the tellings alive by use of gesture, facial expression and body language and, where necessary, story props. Encourage dramatic expression and use of volume, pace, pitch, emphasis and the power of silence. **Plenary** Take the oral stories to another class and give each pair of children a small audience. Invite the audiences to feed back afterwards.	**Speaking and listening:** in pairs one child describes their bedroom to the second child, making it as detailed a description as possible; the second child has to report back to the class one fact or feeling – not a complete recount

DAY 5 ▪ Story starts

Key features	Stages	Additional opportunities
	Introduction Model an exciting 'story start' for the class, for example *Jean woke up. It was very late. The house was quiet and dark and yet... What had woken her?* Discuss the effect this has on the reader, perhaps it generates worry, interest, makes you want to read on. Ask the children what they think the three dots mean?	
Self-awareness: discuss and reflect on their personal responses to the texts	**Speaking and listening** Encourage the children to work in pairs or small groups to create really exciting, powerful story starts for their oral stories from Day 4. Gather the class back together and listen to some of their story starts. Ask the class to comment on: overall effectiveness, vivid descriptions, powerful verbs, connectives.	**Support:** work as a scribe with a group to help them develop and record their own story starts
	Independent work Ask each child to record their own story start, then write it on a piece of paper or large sticky notes.	**Extend:** read the opening chapters of other historical stories and analyse their power
	Plenary Each child should stick their story start on the wall. Ask everyone to walk around and read each other's work. Collect the class back onto the carpet and ask for their opinions about which story starts stick in their mind and why.	

DAY 6 ▪ Story writing

Key features	Stages	Additional opportunities
	Introduction Fleshing out characters – the extract *Simon* on the CD-ROM. What inferences can the children make about the characters. Revisit the 'story mountains' story planning the children developed in previous sessions. Read some of them out to the class. Discuss any improvements or additions that could be made.	
	Independent work Invite the children to write their story using the paragraphs: 1. Beginning (story start already written); 2. Build-up; 3. Climax; 4. Conclusion/resolution. Let the children continue with their writing. Encourage use of paragraphs, strong verbs and the use of connectives to show changes in time.	**Support:** use a box of story props to help develop their story
Creative thinking: create a setting and a new story set in the past	**Plenary** Organise the children into pairs and ask them to read their stories to each other. They should give each other feedback on the links between events and on details to create the historical setting and characters.	**ICT:** word-process their stories then, using a graphics program, illustrate certain points

Guided reading

In groups, read the extracts of *Once There Were Lions* from the CD-ROM and then ask the children to summarise the plot development for each one.

Assessment

Work with each individual child to mark and assess their historical story. Ask them to complete the CD-ROM assessment activity.

The areas to focus on through questioning and discussion are: Can they plan, tell and write a story set in the past? Does their story include detail to evoke the historical setting? Can they sequence events clearly and show how one event leads to another?

Refer back to the learning outcomes on page 11.

Further work

Read more historical stories to the children. Discuss what makes them historical. Give the children copies of passages from the stories and highlighting pens and invite them to highlight, for example, powerful verbs, connectives, adverbs, adjectives.

Name _____   Date _____

Features of historical stories

■ Write notes in the chart below using the two texts you have been studying.

Fact	Inference	Example from the text

100 LITERACY FRAMEWORK LESSONS YEAR 4

Name —————————————————— **Date** ——————————

Characterisation chart

■ Complete the chart with facts from the text.

Character's name	Characteristic	Speech	Relationship with other characters

Facts, inferences and feelings

■ Complete this chart with facts, inferences and feelings from the text to produce a character sketch.

Fact	Inference	Feeling	

PHOTOCOPIABLE ■SCHOLASTIC
www.scholastic.co.uk

Name ————————————— Date —————————————

Story mountain

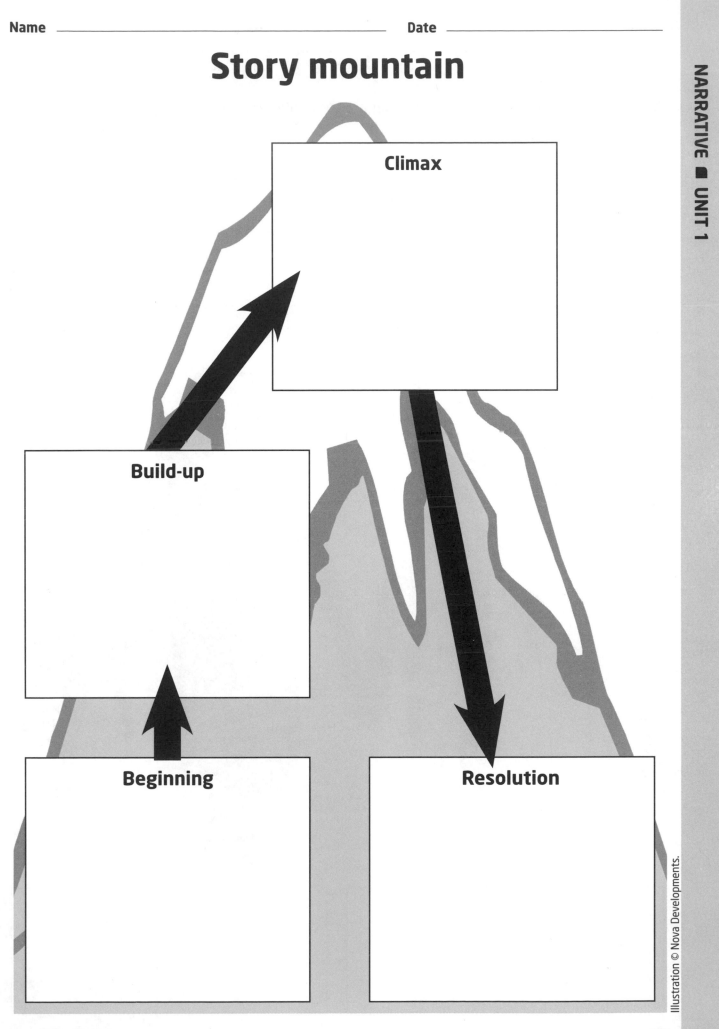

Climax

Build-up

Beginning

Resolution

Into the picture

■ What are these people thinking? What are they saying? Where have they come from? Where are they going?

■ Write some of your ideas in the boxes.

■ 100 LITERACY FRAMEWORK LESSONS YEAR 4

NARRATIVE
UNIT 2 Stories set in imaginary worlds

Speak and listen for a range of purposes on paper and on screen

Strand 1 Speaking
- Tell stories effectively and convey detailed information coherently for listeners.

Read for a range of purposes on paper and on screen

Strand 7 Understanding and interpreting texts
- Explain how writers use figurative and expressive language to create images and atmosphere.

Strand 8 Engaging with and responding to texts
- Read extensively favourite authors/genres and experiment with other types of text.

Write for a range of purposes on paper and on screen

Strand 9 Creating and shaping texts
- Develop and refine ideas in writing using planning and problem-solving strategies.
- Use settings and characterisation to engage readers' interest.
- Show imagination through language used to create emphasis, humour, atmosphere or suspense.

Strand 10 Text structure and organisation
- Organise texts into paragraphs to distinguish between different information, events or processes.
- Use adverbs and conjunctions to establish cohesion within paragraphs.

Strand 11 Sentence structure and punctuation
- Clarify meaning and point of view by using varied sentence structure (phrases, clauses and adverbials).

Strand 12 Presentation
- Use word-processing packages to present written work and continue to increase speed and accuracy in typing.

Progression in narrative

In this year children are moving towards:
- Reviewing the structure and features of adventure stories.
- Identifying examples of figurative and expressive language to build a fuller picture of a character.
- Discussing characters' behaviour and the extent to which it is changed by the imaginary world.
- Collecting evidence from stories to build up a picture of an imagined world; noting examples of descriptive language, talking about the mood or atmosphere they create and making predictions about how characters will behave in such a place.
- Using drama to explore the consequences of introducing new characters to a particular setting.
- Planning and writing a longer adventure story set in an imagined world; organising chapters using the structure: introduction, build-up, climax or conflict, resolution; including detail of the setting, using figurative and expressive language to evoke mood and atmosphere.

UNIT 2 ◀ Stories set in imaginary worlds *continued*

Key aspects of learning covered in this Unit

Reasoning
Children will discuss the influence of settings on characters, using evidence from the text to justify their opinions and referring to wider evidence from their own knowledge and experience.

Evaluation
Children will discuss the success criteria they have devised to evaluate their own written work and give feedback to others.

Self-awareness
Children will discuss and reflect on their personal responses to texts.

Communication
Children will often work collaboratively in pairs and groups. They will communicate outcomes orally, in writing and using other modes and media where appropriate.

Prior learning

Before starting this Unit check that the children can:
■ Identify a range of settings used by authors when discussing stories they have read.
■ Use simple connectives to connect ideas in using simple or compound sentences.
If they need further support please refer to a prior Unit or a similar Unit in Year 3.

Resources

Phase 1:
Ignis by Gina Wilson ✿; *The shining pearl parts 1* and *2* and differentiated version by Jay Mathews ✿; Interactive activity 'Setting, atmosphere and character reaction' ✿; Selection of short stories; Photocopiable page 25 'Story mountain; Photocopiable page 41 'Setting, atmosphere and character reaction'; Photocopiable page 42 'Characters being influenced by atmosphere'; Photocopiable page 43 'My dragon adventure story plan'

Phase 2:
Dragon land parts 1 and *2* by Jay Mathews ✿; *Ignis* by Gina Wilson ✿; 'Fantasy' atmosphere music; Painting and collage materials; Photograph slideshow ✿; Computers and image-editing software; Digital camera; Other dragon stories; Plasticine®; collection of 'magical objects'; Photocopiable page 44 'Adverbs and connectives'

Phase 3:
Photograph slideshow ✿; Story props and musical instruments or CDs (optional); Thesauruses; *Ignis* by Gina Wilson ✿; Favourite story books; Books in various formats and media; Computers and word-processing software; Photocopiable page 43 'My dragon adventure story plan'; Assessment activity 'Story skeleton' ✿

Cross-curricular opportunities

Myths and legends (such as St George and the Dragon)

UNIT 2 ■ Teaching sequence

Phase	Children's objectives	Summary of activities	Learning outcomes
1	I enjoy reading books by the same author. I understand what figurative and expressive language is and know how authors use it. I can use adjectives and similes to make characters come alive. I can plan a dragon story.	Discuss character, setting and plot. Explore a character in a story. Discuss and identify author's use of expressive elements. Develop setting, character and atmosphere in stories. Plan the outline of a dragon story.	Children can express opinions about an author's intended impact on a reader.
2	I can use 'mind walking' to help me get a picture in my head of an imaginary world. I can find out about a character by hot-seating him/her. I can make my own fantasy setting by using a photograph-editing program. I can explain how my altered photographs create different atmospheres. I can create model characters reacting to a background. I can tell stories using my models and backgrounds as story props. I can improve my storytelling techniques.	Enter an imaginary world through 'mind-walking.' Develop settings and characters for a dragon story. Hot-seat Ignis the dragon. Flesh out own dragon characters. Create settings for own stories using a photograph-editing program. Consider the effects of atmosphere created through editing photographs. Develop model characters showing their response to atmospheres. Develop oral versions of own stories. Revisit story skeletons. Prepare and deliver a second oral story.	Children can tell a story orally based on their role play, using the organisational and language features of the text type.
3	I can say what I like and dislike about a story. I can work in a group to plan and write a shared fantasy adventure story. I can use superlative and comparative adjectives. I understand that sentences of different length can create impact in a story. I can work in my group to write the final paragraph to our story. I can publish a story in a variety of different ways. I can plan a story using a flat plan. I understand and can use apostrophes in my writing. I understand what a book blurb does. I can write the blurb for my own story.	Model an exciting dragon story. Discuss likes and dislikes. Tell a shared story orally. Draft a fantasy adventure story. Agree success criteria. Revise story starts. Develop a main character. Write a build-up paragraph. Look at different sentence lengths. Write the climax paragraph. Write conclusion/resolution paragraphs. Show a variety of ways to publish stories. Complete final drafts and check progress. Plan a published story using a flat plan. One-to-one interviews with children to finalise their stories. Revise the rule of apostrophising. Word-process stories. Write the back page blurb. Complete the publishing process.	Children can write a narrative using paragraphs to organise ideas, maintaining cohesion within and between paragraphs.

Provide copies of the objectives for the children.

DAY 1 ■ A character's thoughts and actions

Key features	Stages	Additional opportunities
Reasoning: discuss the influence of settings on characters	**Introduction** Read the extract *Ignis* by Gina Wilson from the CD-ROM. Discuss the character, setting and plot. Display the extract or give children copies to read. Ask the class to discuss: where the action is taking place (the setting); what is in the setting; who is in the setting (character). Display the simple story skeleton photocopiable page 25 'Story mountain' (or draw your own) and work together to recreate the storyline from the extract. **Speaking and listening** Ask the children to act out Ignis' quest while you read the extract again. Stop reading at certain points and freeze the action. Walk around the room 'bringing individual children alive' to hear what they are thinking as the character Ignis (spotlighting) at that moment in the story. **Independent work** Give each child a copy of the story extract, *Ignis,* a blank piece of paper and pencil. Invite them to draw Ignis and search the text for descriptions of his feelings and thoughts. Then they could add speech bubbles and write their thoughts from the 'spotlighting' activity. **Plenary** Display *Ignis* and invite children to come out and underline the words and phrases which describe his character and actions.	**Support:** give a group of children a picture of a dragon and ask them to write some adjectives and adjectival phrases to describe it **Extend:** research dragons on the internet and create a fact and fiction sheet for the class to use

DAY 2 ■ Settings and atmospheres

Key features	Stages	Additional opportunities
Self-awareness: discuss and reflect on their personal response to the texts	**Introduction** Remind the children about story settings and the impact they have on characters. Display the interactive activity 'Setting, atmosphere and character reaction' from the CD-ROM and invite the class to help you drag and drop different settings, atmospheres and character reactions into the appropriate empty boxes and discuss the effects. Now read the story *The shining pearl parts 1* and *2* from the CD-ROM. Ask for the children's response to the story. What elements in the story made it interesting or different? Was its tone spooky? Magical? How did the author evoke the atmosphere? **Speaking and listening** In pairs, ask the children to develop a simple everyday scene between Jade Dragon and Golden Phoenix. Then change an element. How would the characters react? Ask them to note the different things they try on photocopiable page 41 'Setting, atmosphere and character reaction'.	**Support:** use *The shining pearl* differentiated text **Extend:** paint a picture of the Queen of Heaven looking down on Jade Dragon and the Golden Phoenix with the pearl; paint the rays of light stretching up to heaven; on each ray write an adjectival phrase or chain of words to describe the pearl
Communication: work collaboratively in pairs and groups	**Independent work** Organise the class into pairs and give each pair copies of *Ignis* and *The shining pearl* and invite them to complete their own setting – atmosphere – character reaction grid by picking out examples from each of the two story extracts and writing the evidence in the correct columns. **Plenary** Read out some adjectival phrases and similes from *The shining pearl* and ask the children to tell you which character is being described.	

DAY 3 ■ Characters' reactions

Key features	Stages	Additional opportunities
Reasoning: discuss the influence of settings on characters, using evidence from the text to justify opinions and referring to wider evidence from their own knowledge and experience	**Introduction** Read *The shining pearl parts 1* and *2* which gives a good example of characters being influenced by an atmosphere as created by the author. Ask the children if they can identify this in the story. Read the story again and, this time, ask the children to interpret the mood of a character in body language and facial expressions as you read. Remind the children about use of adjectives, adjectival phrases and similes. Look for some examples in the extract. Display the story and invite the children to help you find good examples from the text. **Speaking and listening** Ask groups of children to find an extract from a favourite book and look for the adjectives, adjectival phrases and similes. They could act out these phrases to get a feel for their dramatic qualities. **Independent work** Children could now use chalks on big pieces of sugar paper to create dramatic pictures. Ask them to complete photocopiable page 42 'Characters being influenced by atmosphere' where they write adjectives and similes. **Plenary** Share some of the findings as a class. In pairs, ask the children to think of a simile to describe their partner. Write their contributions on the board.	**Role play:** children create 'consequences cards' on which they write a setting, a character and an atmosphere, they swap cards and perform a simple role play, showing how the setting affects the character

DAY 4 ■ Story planning

Key features	Stages	Additional opportunities
	Introduction Can the children recall the work you did on interpreting character reactions to settings and atmospheres? In a large space, ask the children to walk around, following their own pathways. On a signal from you, they freeze. You then call out a setting, such as a muddy path, for them to respond to by the way they move, react and feel. Freeze the action and 'spotlight' some children to hear what they are thinking: *Oh no I've got my best trainers on – they'll get ruined in all this mud!* Repeat with other settings. **Speaking and listening** Ask the children to sit in a space and close their eyes and think of a fantasy dragon character. Ask them to slowly 'morph' into that character and start to move around the room in character. Freeze the action. Ask them to think about one thing to say in role as their chosen dragon character. Unfreeze the action, ask them to continue moving around the room in character and spotlight some of them. Write their ideas and thoughts on a flipchart.	**Simile:** in a circle one child starts by saying a phrase, child two adds a simile, child three adds to the simile; when the children run out of ideas start a new simile
Communication: work collaboratively in pairs	**Independent work** In pairs, the children decide on their own dragon story plan outline. They should think of their dragon character, the setting and an idea for the event. **Plenary** Together they write a story skeleton using the photocopiable page 43 'My dragon adventure story plan'.	

Guided reading

Read some story extracts and discuss the setting, atmosphere and plot.
Look for clues about how the characters in the stories react to the setting and atmosphere.

Assessment

Read a short story to the children.
Ask them questions: *Who is the main character? Who are the main characters? What is the setting for the story? What atmosphere does the author create? What effect does this have on the main character/ characters?*
Refer back to the learning outcomes on page 29.

Further work

Choose some more stories. Ask the children to work in small groups to discuss the setting, atmosphere and impact on the characters.

DAY 1 ■ Planning our own stories

Key features	Stages	Additional opportunities
Reasoning: discuss the influence of setting on characters	### Introduction The children are going to plan and tell their own dragon adventure story and illustrate it later using photograph-editing techniques. In a large space, lead the class in developing a 'land before time' fantasy landscape. Ask them to lie on the floor with their eyes closed. Play some suitable music and read *Dragon land parts 1* and *2* from the CD-ROM. They should focus their minds and, on command from you, slowly open their eyes and start exploring their fantasy environment. ### Speaking and listening Gather together and collect the children's thoughts, ideas, descriptions and feelings about the environment they have just explored. ### Independent work Organise the class into pairs and invite them to draw on their experiences of fantasy stories to discuss and plan a dragon adventure story of their own. There should only be two characters in the story – the dragon and one other. Encourage them to build up the story plan by settings – characters – atmosphere. They could use the 'Story mountain' skeleton planning grids: beginning, build-up, climax, resolution. ### Plenary Draw the class together and choose one story plan to share with the class. Use a story mountain or other story planning technique on the board.	**Support:** sketch or paint a fantasy setting while listening to the music played during the mind-walking activity **Extend:** as above, then write adjectives, adjectival phrases and similes to describe aspects and elements of the setting

DAY 2 ■ Main characters

Key features	Stages	Additional opportunities
Communication: work in pairs to communicate using writing and other modes	### Introduction In this session, children are going to 'flesh out' the main dragon character for their own story and develop a second character. Read the story extract *Ignis* again. Invite children to hot-seat you (or a confident child) as Ignis to find out more about him, then, in a circle, share their new knowledge and understanding of his character. ### Speaking and listening Challenge pairs of children to invent a second character for their story. Ask them to think about name, character, relationship to the main character. Give each pair a copy of a simple characterisation grid to help them organise their planning, for example: *Name, Physical attributes, Characteristics, Likes/Dislikes, Relationship to other characters.* ### Independent work Ask the children, in pairs, to revisit their own story plans and flesh out their main dragon character and add the second character. Ask them to draw or paint a large picture of their characters and write words and phrases to describe them around the edge. ### Plenary Each pair should introduce their dragon characters to the rest of the class. Invite the children to comment on each other's ideas and give suggestions for the addition of further details.	**Collage dragons:** paint, sponge or roller print a fantasy setting background for a wall display, then create their character either through collage or printing, cut it out and arrange it in the setting
Evaluation: discuss and evaluate; give feedback to others		

DAY 3 ▪ Creating settings and atmospheres

Key features	Stages	Additional opportunities
Self-awareness: discuss and reflect on personal responses to texts **Communication:** work collaboratively to communicate using different media	**Introduction** Tell the children that they are going to create settings for their stories which contain certain atmospheric effects using a photograph-editing program, such as Picasa from Google. Show them the Photograph slideshow on the CD-ROM. Ask the children to comment on the images – what atmosphere does each of them create? Demonstrate how to create the effects (you will need to have tried out the photograph-editing program yourself beforehand). **Independent work** Give each pair their story planning grids from the previous lesson and invite them time to plan and create their own atmospheric backgrounds for their own dragon stories. They should experiment with the photograph-editing program. Either allow the children to take some photographs around the school using digital cameras, or take some before the lesson for class use. Make sure they keep notes about the filters or effects they have used. **Plenary** Ask the pairs to print out one of their attempts to share with the class. Encourage them to describe how they achieved the special effects. Other members of the class should be encouraged to give their comments and ideas for improvements.	**Support:** some children will need the support of an adult in completing this task **Extend:** create their own computer-generated dragon character by cropping two photographs and joining them together; then superimpose their character onto one of their altered settings

DAY 4 ▪ Reacting to atmospheres

Key features	Stages	Additional opportunities
            Self-awareness: discuss and reflect on personal responses to texts	**Introduction** Display the slideshow of 'altered images' from the CD-ROM again and ask the children to discuss the order they are in: a quiet restful one for the beginning, a dramatic one for the climax. Discuss with the children how the atmosphere of the images would make Ignis the dragon feel. How would he react? What might his facial expressions be? How might his body language look? Invite a few children to stand in front of each of the images in a freeze-frame showing their reactions to the atmosphere with their body language and facial expressions. **Speaking and listening** Discuss with the audience their feelings about the freeze-frames. Do they echo their feelings about the altered images? Take digital photographs of the children's freeze-frame in front of the projected images. **Independent work** Leave one of the altered settings on display. Invite all the class, in small groups, to try out the freeze-frame reactions. Each child decides what characteristics their character will have and therefore how they will, individually react – bravado, fear, bursting into tears and so on. **Plenary** 'Bring them alive'. Each group shows in speech and body reactions how they are feeling and reacting to the setting. Write down some of their ideas.	**Support:** look at other settings in books, photographs and paintings, discuss how the main characters are reacting in the pictures **Extend:** develop characters by taking digital photographs of the reaction of each child in their group to the setting and writing a speech bubble (ensure to get parents' or carers' permission before taking photographs)

DAY 5 ■ Dragon stories come alive!

Key features	Stages	Additional opportunities
Self-awareness: discuss and reflect on their personal responses to texts	### Introduction Demonstrate some good story beginnings from other stories (dragon stories if possible). Ask the children to discuss the features of good story starts. ### Speaking and listening Ask the pairs of children to role play the beginning of their story. One child is the dragon character and the other plays the chosen second character. Stop the action and invite some pairs to present their 'beginning' sequence to the class. Continue with the role plays through the build-up, climax and resolution phases.	
Communication: work collaboratively in pairs and groups, communicating outcomes orally, in writing and using other modes and media	### Independent work Let each pair of children mount their altered images onto card and fix them to a wall with a desk/table in front. Image one should represent the beginning of the story, image two represents the build-up, and so on. The pairs then create Plasticine® models of their story characters as they would be at the beginning of their story in front of the first image. If there is time, they could then take a digital photograph of the scene. Allow the children to alter the models to react to the second image – the build-up of their story and take a digital picture of that. Repeat with the climax and resolution images. Help the children to import their images onto the computer as a slideshow. ### Plenary Display an example or two of the children's work. Discuss the effects and how the children have altered the models to show their reaction to the atmosphere of the background.	**Further work:** creating the Plasticine® models might take longer than one session, and might need to continue in groups during the course of the day

DAY 6 ■ My dragon story

Key features	Stages	Additional opportunities
	### Introduction In this session, the children are going to prepare an oral version of their dragon story. Show the children a storytelling program (copyright permitting) where the storyteller is filmed telling the story while still images and animated sequences are superimposed all around.	
	### Speaking and listening Invite the children to help you tell an exciting dragon story enhanced by the Photograph slideshow from the CD-ROM. Use exciting descriptive language, sequencing of events, good adjectival phrases and effective connectives.	**Support:** ask a confident child to work in the group as the main storyteller
Communication: tell a story with the help of different media	### Independent work Challenge the children to practice an oral telling of their dragon story using the digital photographs of their Plasticine models and enhanced altered backgrounds. They should organise their oral storytellings into four paragraphs, such as beginning, build-up, climax, resolution. Move from pair to pair encouraging them to use exciting descriptive language, strong verbs, interesting adjectives and connectives. Invite some pairs to tell their stories to the rest of the class. Encourage positive comments and suggestions for improvement. ### Plenary Ask children to add brief notes to their story planners to remind them of ideas gained from the oral storytelling.	**Extend:** ask a local storyteller/author to come in to tell some dragon stories to the class and to talk about the art of storytelling

DAY 7 ■ Really useful adverbs

Key features	Stages	Additional opportunities
	### Introduction	**Adverbs:** play adverb games, for example act out adverbs for other children to guess
	Tell the class you are going to work on developing more ideas to improve the quality of their stories. Recall the use of similes, powerful verbs, adjectives and connectives. Remind the children about adverbs (words which modify a verb, adjective or another adverb). Display photocopiable page 44 'Adverbs and connectives' from the CD-ROM or give each child a copy to complete. Invite some children to choose adverbs from the word bank and write them in the spaces in the text. Ask volunteers to highlight connectives in the text extract.	
Evaluation: discuss the success criteria devised to evaluate own work	### Speaking and listening	
	Ask the pairs to discuss what makes a good storyteller, for example animated facial and vocal expressions, use of interesting language, pace (pauses, speeding up and so on). Now ask them to revisit their story planning and think of ways to improve the quality of their stories.	
	### Independent work	
	Give the pairs of children their planning and notes about their dragon story which they used to prepare their oral storytelling. Challenge them to add some interesting adverbs to use in a second telling of their story.	
	### Plenary	
	Hold a series of 'dress rehearsals' to enable the pairs to try out their storytellings before going to another class to tell their stories. Invite comments from the audience.	

Guided reading

Ask the group to read a chapter from a book, (preferably a dragon story to keep the theme going). Ask them to look carefully at any page and examine how the author has organised the text. Look at the use of paragraphs. Do they follow a structure of, say, first sentence telling you what the paragraph is about followed by further detail and evidence? Are there key words in the paragraphs to give the reader clues?

Construct a flow chart summary for some of the paragraphs.

Assessment

Organise a storytelling session with another class. Prior to the session, ask children to develop their own success criteria to assess the task, *confident approach, audience listening and interested, use of exciting and interesting language, use of gesture, body language and facial expression, clarity.*

Spend time with each pair and ask them to assess their performance using their own agreed criteria.

Add your own suggestions and ideas for improvement.

Refer back to the learning outcomes on page 29.

Further work

Give a group of children some 'magical objects', for example: a string of sparkling beads, a tiara, a sparkling stone. Ask them for words and phrases to describe their objects.

Invite the children to make up a simple story using the 'magic objects' as stimuli. Suggest they organise their stories into sections in readiness for a storytelling session for a younger group of children.

DAY 1 ■ Modelling writing

Key features	Stages	Additional opportunities
Self-awareness: discuss and reflect on their personal responses to the texts	### Introduction In Phase 3, the children are going to use their skills, experiences and gathered words and phrases developed in Phase 2 (the oral storytelling), to bring to an exciting adventure fantasy story based on their oral stories. Model a simple story on the board using four paragraphs (beginning, build-up, climax, resolution). Either use the four altered photographs provided on the CD-ROM or prepare your own. Use this activity as an opportunity to recap on the activities undertaken in Phases 1 and 2, including setting, characterisation, plot, how characters react to the atmosphere created by the author and the illustrator, use of conjunctives, adverbs, strong verbs and similes. ### Speaking and listening Encourage groups to discuss what they think about the finished story. Does it make an impact? Why? Why not? What could they add to it? Ask a spokesperson in each group to feed back to the class on behalf of the group. ### Independent work What makes a great story? Ask children to prepare book reviews (ideally about dragons) to share with the rest of the class. ### Plenary Ask the children to analyse what it is about their chosen story they like/dislike. Can they give examples to back-up their viewpoint?	**Support:** draw pictures of their favourite part of a story and write a sentence underneath explaining why they like it **Extend:** devise a questionnaire for other children to find out their favourite stories and what it is they particularly like about them

DAY 2 ■ Shared writing

Key features	Stages	Additional opportunities
	### Introduction Remind the children about the shared story you created together on Day 1. Ask the children to create a shared version of a dragon story, perhaps St George and the Dragon. Who is the intended audience? Give groups time to discuss the story content. Scribe their ideas on photocopiable page 43 'My dragon adventure story plan'. ### Speaking and listening In small groups, prepare an oral telling of the planned story in four sections. The groups could use story props and music to create atmosphere. ### Independent work The children are going to write the first paragraph (the beginning) of their own dragon adventure fantasy story. They will need their story planning sheets and altered images from Phase 2. Ensure they introduce a character and describe a setting (including place, weather, time of day or season to help create an atmosphere). Check they include powerful verbs and use adjectives and adverbs effectively. ### Plenary Work with the class on developing an agreed success criteria for the story writing exercise. Think about the story writing aspects covered in this Unit: structure, character development, characters influenced by setting, use of strong verbs, connectives, similes, adverbs, adjectives and so on.	**Support:** read some of children's paragraphs. Write up some descriptive words from the paragraphs and ask children to suggest alternatives **Extend:** ask groups to check progress against the agreed success criteria for this task; How do they think they are progressing? What evidence is there for this?

Communication: work collaboratively in pairs

Evaluation: discuss the success criteria they have devised to evaluate their own written work

DAY 3 ■ Story build-up

Key features	Stages	Additional opportunities
	Introduction Choose a good example of a beginning 'dragon story' paragraph. Discuss how the paragraphs relate to each other. Look at the use of connectives and adjectives. Display a version of the example prepared with a selection of connectives and adjectives to drop into gaps in the text. Invite children to drop suitable connectives and adjectives into the gaps.	
Communication: work collaboratively in different media	**Speaking and listening** Organise the class into pairs, with a thesaurus. Ask them to pick a character from one of their stories, draw a picture and write a description underneath using comparative and superlative adjectives. Encourage the children to use language to encourage readers to like or dislike the character.	**Support:** give a group a sheet of adjectives and invite them to add the comparative and superlative for them **Extend:** create some character sketches which intend to make the reader either dislike or like the character; try them out on some other children and ask for their reactions
	Independent work Encourage the children to look again at their beginning paragraphs and add/change anything in light of the activities undertaken above. Now ask them to write the first draft of their second paragraph, the build-up of their story, using their story mountain/skeletons from Phase 2.	
	Plenary Read a child's paragraph, leaving out some of the descriptions. Ask the class to suggest some adjectives to fill the gaps.	

DAY 4 ■ Story climax

Key features	Stages	Additional opportunities
Reasoning: discuss the influence of settings on characters	**Introduction** In this session the children will look at different length sentences and consider the effect this creates in the impact of the narrative, for example short sentences to regain reader's attention and when something exciting happens, longer ones to describe atmosphere and build tension before writing the first draft of their story climax paragraph. Read the extract from *Ignis* by Gina Wilson from the CD-ROM and analyse the length of each sentence and the way it impacts on the story climax.	**Support:** role play a scenario when one child has received some fantastic news; every sentence has to be short and excited **Extend:** role play a scenario in threes, one child as a narrator; use short sentences to give pace and long sentences to describe the setting
	Speaking and listening Give each pair of children a copy of the extract and invite them to read it dramatically, using excited voices, animated facial expressions and body language.	
	Independent work Now the children can spend some time writing a first draft of their individual story 'climax' paragraph. Encourage a build-up of suspense and use of different-length sentences to add pace and impact.	
Evaluation: discuss the success criteria they have devised to give feedback to others	**Plenary** In small groups, ask the children to share their story climax paragraphs and offer suggestions to improve the excitement and tension. Use the agreed success criteria developed on Day 2. Share each group's thoughts and ideas. Did children find it helpful to have other people's suggestions and advice? Did anything actually change their mind about the way they have written their 'climax' paragraph?	

DAY 5 ■ Conclusions and resolutions

Key features	Stages	Additional opportunities
	Introduction Look together at some story conclusions and resolutions. What makes them effective?	**Support:** draw a picture of the end of their story and write some descriptive phrases around it
Communication: communicate outcomes orally	**Speaking and listening** In small groups, some children could tell each other the endings to their stories, adding some of the emotions and effects described above.	
	Independent work Children should now feel confident to write their final paragraph, trying to create some of the atmosphere.	**Extend:** gather together some final words from favourite story books and make a class phrase bank to help other children
	Plenary Read some of the story endings, missing out adjectives. Ask the children to add some of their own.	

DAY 6 ■ Types of books

Key features	Stages	Additional opportunities
	Introduction This session will help the children decide how to publish their story. Provide a variety of texts, for example digital book, a spiral-bound book, pop-up book, hardback book, picture book, paperback.	
	Speaking and listening Discuss the merits of different styles of books. For example hardbacked books last a long time, picture books are easy to read.	**Support:** produce a story strip
Evaluation: discuss the success criteria devised to evaluate own written work	**Independent work** Children should tidy up their final drafts and check spelling and grammar.	
	Plenary Check children's progress against the class success criteria chart.	

DAY 7 ■ Flat plans

Key features	Stages	Additional opportunities
	Introduction Demonstrate how to produce a simple 'flat plan' using the 'table' tab in WORD: a series of small boxes each one representing a page in the finished book.	**Support:** design an advert for their story; use exciting, enticing adjectives and phrases
Self-awareness: discuss and reflect	**Speaking and listening** Look at and discuss published books to learn about format: cover, inside cover, contents, dedications, pages back to back, space for illustrations.	
	Independent work Let children create their own flat plan showing the format of their story.	**Extend:** visit a printing company to look at the processes involved in printing a book
	Plenary Meet with each child individually, reviewing their story, checking spellings, paragraphs, connectives and so on.	

DAY 8 ■ The publishing process

Key features	Stages	Additional opportunities
	Introduction Check that the children are secure with the rule of apostrophising. Marking possession: singular nouns; plural nouns ending in *s*; irregular plural nouns and omission.	**Apostrophe:** make a simple funny role play to demonstrate the use of the apostrophe, call it 'The misunderstood apostrophe'
	Speaking and listening Ask children, in pairs to check out the use of apostrophes in their stories.	
Self-awareness: discuss and reflect on their personal responses to the text	**Independent work** Children write their stories on the computer with the images created in Phase 2 and adding some more illustrations of the characters by scanning their own drawings or using more altered images. Those who finish early could be 'editors' to proofread other people's stories.	
	Plenary Swap stories and discuss effective strategies used and one area of the narrative that needs a stronger link between ideas.	

DAY 9 ■ Back page blurb

Key features	Stages	Additional opportunities
Self-awareness: discuss and reflect on their personal responses to the text	**Introduction** What job does the 'blurb' on the back page of a book do? For example it makes us want to read the book, gives us a synopsis of the story.	**Support:** an adult might need to help some children with their word-processing
	Speaking and listening Give children a selection of books and ask them to read the back page blurbs and discuss their effectiveness.	
	Independent work Invite the children to write and design the back cover (including blurb) for their own books. Allow them to spend time completing the stories in their published format.	**Extend:** role play as literary critics for a large newspaper; interview children, take notes and create a simple newspaper report using a word-processing package
	Plenary Display all the books and invite the class to walk around and read some of them. Ask the children to give their opinions about one of the stories, explaining why they like it and giving examples from it.	

Guided reading
Read *Ignis* by Gina Wilson. Did the children enjoy the story? Can they explain why? (Think about the variety of author skills discussed in Phase 3.) Does the story flow coherently? Can they explain how? (Use of connectives.)

Assessment
Use the interactive story skeleton from the CD-ROM and invite the children to plan a story on a theme chosen by you which maintains cohesion between the paragraphs. Refer back to the learning outcomes on page 29.

Further work
Invite a storyteller or author into the class to talk to the children about how she/he writes stories and poems. Ask the children to compile questions to ask the author.

Setting, atmosphere and character reaction

Name _____ Date _____

■ Make a note of the different elements you use while developing your scene.

Setting	Atmosphere	Character reaction

Setting		Atmosphere	Character reaction	
Caribbean island	Crystal clear sea	Dark, windy night	Shock	Anger
Scottish mountain	Spooky house	Bright, sunny day	Fear	Desperation
Crowded city street	Prison	Storm brewing	Happiness	Nervousness
Beach	Deep forest	Thick snow storm	Excitement	Apprehension
Train journey	Rush hour	Thunder and lightning	Anticipation	Confusion
Countryside		Impending invasion or war	Anxiety	Frustration
Aeroplane journey		Misty morning	Peacefulness	
Sandy desert		People fighting and shouting	Awe and wonder	

Characters being influenced by atmosphere

Character's name:	
Adjectives or adjectival phrases	
Simile	

Character's name:	
Adjectives or adjectival phrases	
Simile	

Character's name:	
Adjectives or adjectival phrases	
Simile	

■ 100 LITERACY FRAMEWORK LESSONS YEAR 4

PHOTOCOPIABLE  ■■SCHOLASTIC
www.scholastic.co.uk

My dragon adventure story plan

Setting	Character	Atmosphere

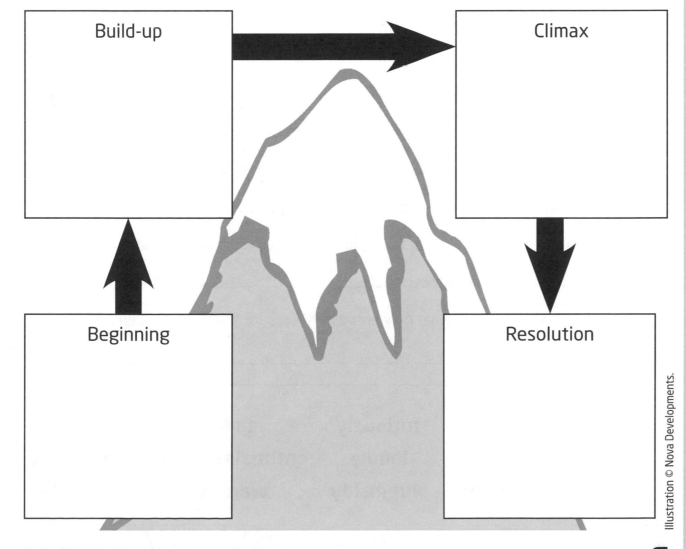

Build-up

Climax

Beginning

Resolution

Illustration © Nova Developments.

Adverbs and connectives

■ Write your ideas for missing adverbs into the spaces using the words at the bottom of the page.

■ Highlight the connective words and phrases.

The storm did not last all night and the thunder rolled _____ over

the village and blew itself out before the dawn appeared _____ on

the horizon. The rain that had poured on the houses and the street had stopped but it

had made large puddles on the ground. The day broke with bright sunshine and in the

little cottage at the furthest end of the village - closest to the gates of the house on

the hill - it streamed _____ through the crack in the thin curtains of

Jack's bedroom.

Jack stirred as the light fell _____ on his face and he opened his

eyes. The warmth made him feel sleepy and he _____ shut them

and tried to return to his wonderful dream. He had been with his parents and they

were _____ on their way back to their house from a day in the park.

Jack had played games _____ with his father and his mother had

made a delicious picnic. In the afternoon he had played _____ with

his kite that they had bought him for his birthday. They were laughing as they walked

down the street and sang silly songs _____ that his mother had

made up and he knew that what he wanted most was for the day not to end.

quickly	**easily**	**furiously**	**sadly**	**miserably**
happily	**excitedly**	**loudly**	**enthusiastically**	**cautiously**
nervously	**slowly**	**sluggishly**	**warmly**	**brightly**

NARRATIVE
UNIT 3 Stories from other cultures

Speak and listen for a range of purposes on paper and on screen

Strand 1 Speaking
- Use and reflect on some ground rules for sustaining talk for interactions.

Strand 2 Listening and responding
- Identify how talk varies with age, familiarity, gender and purpose.

Strand 4 Drama
- Create roles showing how behaviour can be interpreted from different viewpoints.

Read for a range of purposes on paper and on screen

Strand 7 Understanding and interpreting texts
- Identify and summarise evidence from a text to support a hypothesis.
- Deduce characters' reasons for behaviour from their actions and explain how ideas are developed in non-fiction texts.
- Explain how writers use figurative and expressive language to create images and atmosphere.

Strand 8 Engaging with and responding to texts
- Read extensively favourite authors/genres and experiment with other types of text.
- Interrogate texts to deepen and clarify understanding and response.
- Explore why and how writers write, including through face-to-face and online contact with authors.

Write for a range of purposes on paper and on screen

Strand 10 Text structure and organisation
- Organise texts into paragraphs to distinguish between different information, events or processes.

Strand 11 Sentence structure and punctuation
- Use commas to mark clauses and the apostrophe for possession.

Progression in narrative

In this year children are moving towards:
- Reviewing the structure and features of different types of story, such as traditional tales, contemporary stories in the context of reading stories from other cultures.
- Discussing the customs and beliefs of the culture that a story is from and the way that this affects characters' behaviour and actions.
- Making predictions about actions and consequences and discuss whether characters behaved in expected or unexpected ways. Make deductions about characters' motives and feelings.
- Looking at the way that descriptive language and small details are used to build an impression of an unfamiliar place; making predictions about how characters will behave in such a setting.
- Working in role to 'interview' story characters.
- Retelling a traditional tale from another culture using techniques to entertain the audience: gestures, repetition, traditional story openings and endings.
- Noting responses to texts in a reading journal.

▶

Key aspects of learning covered in this Unit

Communication
Make connections and see relationships.
Managing feelings
Recognise, label and think about their feelings.
Empathy
Direct others or follow the directions of others.
Recognise similarities and differences between themselves and others.
Motivation
Carry out an activity to achieve an anticipated outcome.
Take an interest in, watch and listen to other people.
Problem Solving
Look at and think about things differently and from other points of view.
Evaluation
Express their own views, opinions and preferences.

Prior learning

Before starting this Unit check that children can:
■ Recognise settings in stories that are familiar to them.
■ Make some inferences from texts read.
If they need further support please refer to a prior Unit or a similar Unit in Year 3.

Resources

Phase 1:
The girl parts 1 and *2* by Roger Hurn ✾; *Facts about Vietnam* by Jay Mathews ✾; Reference books and brochures about Vietnam; Reading journals; Stories from various cultures; World map; Photocopiable page 58 'Expressive language'
Phase 2:
The ghostly woman by Roger Hurn ✾; Another similar story; Photocopiable page 59 'Figurative language'
Phase 3:
Gran comes to visit parts 1 and *2* by Jay Mathews (including differentiated version) ✾; A favourite book and, if possible, access to the author; Traditional tales from various cultures; Circle time toy; Photocopiable page 60 'Asking questions'; Photocopiable page 61 'Paragraphs and apostrophes'; Photocopiable page 62 'The day the sky was illuminated by a bonfire'; Assessment activity 'Story review' ✾

Cross-curricular opportunities

RE: looking at different religions
PSHE (SEAL): personal beliefs and cultures
Geography: study of different countries

UNIT 3 ■ Teaching sequence

Phase	Children's objectives	Summary of activities	Learning outcomes
1	I can describe what I like about a story. I can tell when a story is from a different culture. I know what makes a story effective. I can find out facts about the background of a story. I can compare my life with that of characters in stories. I can take part in a role play to show the difference between how a character acts and feels. I understand that readers enjoy a story more if they know some facts about the setting. I can review a story. I can take part in a class debate and argue for or against a motion.	Read a story from Vietnam. Predict outcomes. Look for clues to show the story is not from the UK. Detect interesting and expressive language. Look in detail at the organisation *The girl.* Research lifestyles, culture and beliefs of people in Vietnam. Discuss own belief system, compare with that of people in another country. Make oral presentations. Use reading journals to write a book review. Prepare and participate in a full formal class debate.	Children can read stories from other cultures. Children know how paragraphs or chapters are used to collect, order and build-up ideas. Children know how a story is organised through paragraphs, connectives and sentence length. Children can discuss characters and compare customs and beliefs from different cultures.
2	I can predict what happens next in a story and take part in a role play to show my ideas. I understand how setting affects characters. I can find examples of figurative and expressive language. I can write describing how I feel about characters in a story.	Predict what happens next in a similar genre of story from another culture. Examine how story setting affects characters. Look for examples of figurative and expressive language. Write personal responses to a story.	Children can predict outcomes.
3	I know how to find information, ask questions and write a summary of my findings. I can ask questions to find out more about a character. I can ask questions of the author. I know the difference between formal and informal language. I can tell a story using formal and informal language. I can role play a character using informal or formal speech. I understand how to use clichés and expressions.	Prepare and ask questions to find out how a character is thinking and feeling. Present facts to prove or disprove a hypothesis. Develop questioning skills and enquiry techniques to help deduce characters' actions and feelings. Write to or meet the author and ask him/her questions. Look at informal and formal language and the role the apostrophe of possession . Read and retell a story using formal and informal language. Role-play telephone conversations to distinguish between formal and informal. Look at clichés and expressions.	Children can devise and ask questions. Children can explore different types of talk, for example between characters of different ages. Children can identify how speech can change depending on age. Children can compare informal and formal language.

Provide copies of the objectives for the children.

DAY 1 ◼ A story from Vietnam

Key features	Stages	Additional opportunities
Communication: make connections and see relationships	**Introduction** Read the story, *The girl parts 1* and *2* from the CD-ROM, without the subtitle. Do the children think this story is based in the UK or in another country? What clues are there in the text? Discuss the children's feelings about the story. Was the girl really a ghost? What evidence is there in the story to show that she was (the last sentence)? What genre is the story? Did the children like the story? Why? Talk about the author's use of expressive language. **Speaking and listening** Give groups of children cards with some of the phrases from the story on them. Ask the children to interpret them in movement or freeze-frames for example: *...people were looking up at the sky and hurrying for shelter... ...she looked so forlorn and sad...* **Independent work** Give each pair of children a copy of *The girl parts 1* and *2* and photocopiable page 58 'Expressive language'. Challenge them to highlight examples of expressive language and to pick out: 1. Clues about the story being set in another country, for example *the banyan tree, the air thick and hot.* 2. Adjectives and adjectival phrases, such as *black clouds smothered the sinking sun.* 3. Powerful verbs, such as *trickled, hunched, chuckled, dashed, wobbled.* **Plenary** Share the evidence compiled. Write the ideas under headings, *Evidence of the story's origin, Adjectives/adjectival sentences, Powerful verbs.*	**Support:** provide support when analysing the text for expressive grammar **Extend:** give children paints or chalks and ask them to draw big, bold images to interpret certain words and phrases

DAY 2 ◼ What makes a good story?

Key features	Stages	Additional opportunities
Managing feelings: recognise, label and think about their feelings	**Introduction** Display the story, *The girl* from the CD-ROM and read parts 1 and 2 again with the class. The object of this session is to look in detail at the organisation of a story – what makes it effective. Focus on use of paragraphs – what is contained in each? How are the paragraphs connected (connectives)? Evidence of different-length sentences and how these are used, such as *It had been a long but profitable day* (short sentence enticing the reader to read on to find out why it had been profitable). Notice examples of characters saying one thing but feeling another. **Speaking and listening** Ask the children to think about occasions when they have felt one way inside but showed another emotion to the outside world, such as not being picked to play in the football team, feeling upset but showing a brave face. Role play examples with the children. Spotlight them to hear what they are thinking. **Independent work** In small groups prepare a facts and inferences chart from this story, for example, fact: the girl looked at the taxi driver with large sad eyes; inference: the girl is lonely and wants to see her mum one last time. **Plenary** Can the children empathise with the feelings of the characters in the story?	**Emotions:** think of a scenario where they have felt one way but acted another way; draw two inside/outside pictures showing the outside face and the inside feeling. Add speech bubbles to show readers how they were feeling in this situation

DAY 3 ■ Researching

Key features	Stages	Additional opportunities
	Introduction Explain that children might have a deeper understanding of *The girl* if they have more background information about Vietnam, the culture and beliefs. Display the sheet, *Facts about Vietnam* from the CD-ROM and read it through with the class.	
Empathy: direct others or follow the directions of others	**Independent work** Make available some reference books, holiday brochures and so on and invite children in groups to research their own facts about Vietnam. Before they start their research, ask them to organise themselves to take specific roles within the group. Some children could use the internet. Prepare a large research chart on the wall or board. Sections could include: people, lifestyle, beliefs, history (war between North and South Vietnam in the 1960s), food and crops. Give each group sticky notes. Instruct them to write each fact on a separate note and stick them on the relevant section of the chart.	**Support:** use the fact sheet used in the introduction and highlight interesting facts
Motivation: carry out an activity to achieve an anticipated outcome	**Speaking and listening** Invite the groups to compile a short presentation for the rest of the class. Encourage everyone in each group to participate in some way. **Plenary** Bring the class back together and watch the group presentations. Encourage the audience to ask questions and make positive comments and suggestions.	**Extend:** a group could specifically look for images of Vietnam and create a simple slideshow to present to the rest of the class

DAY 4 ■ What do we think?

Key features	Stages	Additional opportunities
	Introduction Here the children will use the information from the previous session to make a comparison between their own lifestyles and beliefs and those of people living in Vietnam. Show the fact sheet about Vietnam again.	
Empathy: recognise similarities and differences between themselves and others **Motivation:** take an interest in, watch and listen to other people	**Speaking and listening** In pairs, ask children to discuss their own belief systems. List the different belief systems represented within your class. Invite children to explain the basics of their beliefs and the impact this has on their lifestyle. Now ask each child to draw their self-portrait and annotate it with an introduction to themselves, their beliefs and their lifestyle. Encourage them to read their work to the rest of the group. Remind them to speak clearly and think of ways to make their presentation interesting to hold the audience.	**Support:** an adult could take a small group to experience first-hand the place of worship of a particular religious group
	Independent work Describe a scenario where there is a misunderstanding between two friends, both of whom interpret a situation from a different viewpoint. For example: Amanda invites Esther to her birthday tea one Friday after school. Esther wants to come but she can't because she is Jewish and Friday is her special family day. She doesn't explain her situation to Amanda and Amanda feels very hurt, thinking Esther doesn't care about her. Create this or similar role-play scenes in pairs.	**Extend:** ask some children to be reporters and interview another pair in role as their characters from the role-play scenarios in the independent activity
	Plenary Watch then discuss some of the scenarios. Can the children think of stories where characters interpret behaviour from their own perspective?	

DAY 5 ■ Journal writing

Key features	Stages	Additional opportunities
	Introduction Recap on the work undertaken so far in this Unit. The children have analysed a short story from another culture, researched the culture itself and reflected on the similarities and differences between themselves and that culture. Now they are going to use this information in a piece of writing recording their response to the story, *The girl*. Read the story again. Ask the children if their feelings or thoughts about the story have changed now they have more knowledge about the Vietnamese culture and have looked 'in depth' into the facts and inferences within the story.	**Support:** draw a picture of one of the characters and write words and phrases around the outside explaining their feelings
	Speaking and listening Invite a child to answer questions in role as one of the characters from the story to give them more insight into how he/she was feeling.	
Evaluation: express their own views, opinions and preferences	**Independent work** Ask the children to write a review of the story, *The girl* in their reading journals. Ask them to plan it first using a simple writing skeleton, for example: introduction, outline of the story, personal response to the story using quotes from the text and a personal experience, if applicable.	**Extend:** read a different story from another culture and write a comparison review in their reading journals
	Plenary Ask some children to read their reviews and discuss their ideas with the class.	

DAY 6 ■ Do you believe in ghosts?

Key features	Stages	Additional opportunities
	Introduction Tell the class you are going to hold a debate between a group of scientists who don't believe in ghosts and a society of people who do. The children are going to role play the people on both sides of the debate.	
Problem solving: look at and think about things differently and from other points of view	**Speaking and listening** Set up a room with a table and three chairs at the front, and rows of chairs divided into two halves facing the front. One half of the class will be the scientists and the other half the ghost support society. In role as the organiser, call the 'debate' to order. Introduce each group then tell them that they are going to spend some time in their groups deciding on the points of their arguments and who is going to lead each group and be the main spokesperson.	**Support:** take adult support when presenting their arguments for or against the motion under debate
	Independent work The groups spend time planning their argument for or against. One person in each group is elected as the scribe to write the ideas down.	**Extend:** write a persuasive argument in favour of or against the existence of ghosts
	Speaking and listening As organiser, reconvene the meeting and propose the motion. Each group's leader joins you at the front table to open the debate then you open the debate to the floor so that everyone can have their say.	
	Plenary Review the debate. What went well? What could have been better?	

Guided reading

Ask children to read aloud another story from another culture. Choose one which has good illustrations which enhance the atmosphere and message of the story. Work together to think about what makes it interesting and effective. As they read, encourage the children to think about what grabs their attention.

Observe, prompt and praise.

Return to the story and look together at the illustrations. Are there pictures photographs, drawings or paintings? What messages do the illustrations convey?

Assessment

Give a group of children a short story from another culture to read. Invite them to comment on their feelings about the story, the characters and so on. What clues are there to indicate that this story is not set in the UK? Ask them to compile a list of questions and comments they would like to ask the author if he/she were to be there with them.

Read through and comment on their ideas.

Refer back to the learning outcomes on page 47.

Further work

Compile a class collection of stories from other cultures. Invite children to be book reviewers and write their reviews on the stories, giving their personal feelings supported by examples from the texts. Produce a 'stories from other cultures' display. Place a map of the world on the wall. Ask the children to choose a favourite character from one of the stories, draw a large picture of him/her, and write a character sketch to display underneath. These should be stuck around the map with ribbons pinned from the country of origin to the relevant character.

DAY 1 ■ Predictions

Key features	Stages	Additional opportunities
	### Introduction Read the class *The ghostly woman* from the CD-ROM. Stop reading when you reach the line, *Dad and granddad scrambled out of the car and set off to find her...* Ask the children to predict what might happen next in the story.	**Support:** tell the children a well-known fairy story; stop at a certain point and ask them to tell you what is going to happen next
Managing feelings: recognise, label and think about their feelings	### Speaking and listening Ask the class, in small groups, to create a role-play scenario to show what they think might happen next in the story and how they think they might respond if they were in the same situation as the stranded family. Invite some groups to perform their scenes to the rest of the class. Invite the viewers to comment on good use of expressive language and characters' reactions to the setting.	**Extend:** find some facts about Malta and develop a simple presentation for the rest of the class
Problem solving: look at and think about things differently and from other points of view	### Independent work Encourage the children to write a short description about what happened next and how they would feel in a similar situation to the characters in the story as developed in the role play.	
	### Plenary Read some of the children's responses. Draw attention to good examples of figurative and expressive language.	

DAY 2 ■ Figurative language

Key features	Stages	Additional opportunities
	### Introduction Read *The ghostly woman* again. Ask the children to think about how the settings in the story affect the characters, for example the dark stormy conditions making Mum nervous and twitchy, the branches scratching the sides of the car making Anthony feel very frightened. In pairs, look at the illustration from the story and discuss how the illustration makes them feel.	
	### Speaking and listening Ask the children to develop some of their own descriptions about the setting as: 1. simile, for example *the car's headlights sliced through the darkness like a knife through butter*. 2. alliteration: *the tall tragic woman*.	**Support:** provide adult support for completing the photocopiable sheet
Motivation: carry out an activity to achieve an anticipated outcome	### Independent work Give pairs of children copies of the text and a copy of the photocopiable page 59 'Figurative language'. Talk through the definitions of the terms used, such as *metaphor – comparing two things by using one kind of object in place of another to suggest the likeness between them*. Ask them to read the story again on their own looking for examples of the author creating an atmosphere through figurative language, and to write one example for each from the text onto their chart.	**Extend:** give children another story and the photocopiable and ask them to find examples of figurative language in the story
	### Plenary Display the 'Figurative language' chart. Invite children to suggest good examples from their own charts.	

DAY 3 ■ Response to a story

Key features	Stages	Additional opportunities
	Introduction Remind the class about their investigations into the effective use of language in creating the atmosphere for a story and how the characters in the story responded to that atmosphere. In this session, the children are going to write their feelings about the story, *The ghostly woman*.	
Communication: make connections and see relationships	**Speaking and listening** Invite the children, in pairs, to hot-seat each other as the ghostly woman to find out what happened to her in her life perhaps she and her family had been killed in this same place many years before; maybe the woman isn't a ghost at all but a local person who was just passing by, being 'in the right place at the right time'.	**Support:** an adult might need to help some children with the hot-seating **Extend:** invite a confident child to role play an author and others to ask him/her questions about the stories, *The ghostly woman* and *The girl*
Problem solving: look at and think about things differently and from other points of view	**Independent work** Ask the children to write their response to the story in their reading journals. Encourage them to give their opinions about the way the setting influences the characters' feelings and actions, their personal thoughts about how they would react in the same situation and their ideas about the motives of the 'ghostly woman'.	
	Plenary Discuss the children's feelings about the story, and their ideas about who or what the ghostly woman was.	

Guided reading
Give a group of children copies of the two stories read in this Unit so far.
Ask them to work together to compare the stories and find some similarities and differences between them.
One child can be scribe.
Invite each group to report back to the class about their findings.

Assessment
Provide each child with some pictures which conjure up strong feelings, such as fear, disgust, amusement, awe.
Ask them to choose their favourite, then to write (or discuss with you individually) a descriptive passage about the feelings and emotions evoked by their chosen picture.
Refer back to the learning outcomes on page 47.

Further work
Give a pair of children an image which creates a certain atmosphere and evokes strong, easily identifiable emotions.
Invite them to use this image to create a simple story skeleton for their own ghost story.

DAY 1 ■ Hypothesising and questioning

Key features	Stages	Additional opportunities
	Introduction Ask children to work in pairs. Child A talks about themselves while child B listens carefully. Now ask child B to choose one aspect of their partner's talk they found interesting and which posed a question in their mind, for example child A was given a very lively puppy for her birthday. Choose an example and demonstrate how to create a hypothesis, for example the family might find the puppy hard to handle. Ask the class to compile questions which aim to find out more information to support or disprove the hypothesis.	**Support:** give the children some question words to help them compose questions
Motivation: take an interest in, watch and listen to other people	**Speaking and listening** Read *Gran comes to visit parts 1* and *2* from the CD-ROM. Suggest the hypothesis to the children that Gran is really quite homesick. Challenge them to find some clues in the text which give the reader this message. Ask them to write their findings down then share them with a partner. Ask children to prepare some questions for Gran as a hot-seating exercise. Organise the class into pairs, one hot-seating the other as Gran.	**Extend:** create an 'all about...' frieze about the character chosen for the hot-seating exercise; draw a big image of the character then invite children to write facts and feelings on sticky notes and stick them around the picture
	Independent work Invite each child to write a summary of the evidence which has been found about Gran being homesick – stating clearly which information is from the text extract and which came from the hot-seating exercise.	
	Plenary Share some of the summaries and discuss the children's findings together.	

DAY 2 ■ Making deductions

Key features	Stages	Additional opportunities
	Introduction Remind the class about questioning skills and how to gather information about characters and what has influenced them to think and behave in certain ways. Display photocopiable page 60 'Asking questions' and explain how to complete it: name of character, deductions about character from the text and the illustration, what else to find out, what questions to ask to find the information.	**Support:** watch some examples of interviews; encourage the group to think about the techniques used by the interviewer
Problem solving: look at and think about things differently and from other points of view	**Speaking and listening** Choose a favourite book and pick a character. (Try to choose one where the author is accessible either online or to come in for an author visit.) What can the children deduce from the text to help them develop an understanding of the way the character thinks and feels? Encourage children to think of some questions they would like to ask the author about the character they created within the story.	**Extend:** ask each pair to create a freeze-frame; 'spotlight' some characters to hear what they are thinking and feeling; Can the other children guess who the story character is each time?
	Independent work Ask the children to complete the photocopiable sheet about their chosen character. Invite them to write or email some questions to the author. If possible, arrange for the author to come to school for a visit, so that the class can ask their questions directly to him/her.	
	Plenary Ask certain children to explain what they already knew about their chosen character, what they wanted to find out, and the questions they asked.	

DAY 3 ▪ Formal and informal language

Key features	Stages	Additional opportunities
	Introduction Talk to the children about formal and informal language and when we use one rather than another. For example: two friends chatting in the playground will use informal language (*she's*); the same children would use more formal language when presenting their work in assembly or being interviewed to go to secondary school or for a job (*she is*). Together search the text for examples of possessive apostrophes and apostrophes of omission for example omission *won't* (will not); possessive – *the girl's book* (the book of the girl). Display a list of words with apostrophes and ask the children to group them under two headings, *Omission* and *Possession*.	**Support:** some children can use the *Gran comes to visit* differentiated text
	Independent work Give children photocopiable page 61 'Paragraphs and apostrophes', a page of text which has the paragraphs and apostrophes omitted. Ask them to decide where the paragraphs should be and also to add apostrophes of omission and possession so the text makes sense.	
Problem solving: look at and think about things differently and from other points of view	**Plenary** Divide the class into halves. Members of each half then pair up. One half of the class creates a simple role play entitled, 'Tea with the Queen.' They should use formal, polite language. Each child should only have one or two lines of dialogue. The pairs in the other half of the class create a role play entitled, 'Tea with my friend,' using informal language. Watch some of the performances together and invite children's comments on the differences. Write examples of each type of speech on the board.	**Extend:** small groups plan and film a short video scene from their improvised scenes, 'Tea with the Queen' and 'Tea with my friend'

DAY 4 ▪ Dreamtime stories

Key features	Stages	Additional opportunities
	Introduction Read *Gran comes to visit parts 1* and *2* from the CD-ROM. Remind the class about the use of formal and informal language. There are examples of both in this story extract. Can the children find them? For example: the formal storytelling style at the beginning compared with the informal style when Bunda comes home and interacts with Gran.	**Support:** use the *Gran comes to visit* differentiated text; tell the story together as a group
Empathy: recognise similarities and differences between themselves and others	**Speaking and listening** Tell the class that Gran told Bunda a story from the Aboriginal dreamtime every night at bedtime. Ask each child to imagine they are Gran telling Bunda the story 'The day the sky was illuminated by a bonfire' from photocopiable page 62. Give children in small groups a copy of the story. In their group they should read the story, then organise themselves to present an oral retelling. Encourage them to think about the difference between formal and informal language: the narrator could use formal language while several others could be acting the parts in the story and use normal informal speech.	**Extend:** look at some images from the internet and rewrite the Aboriginal dreamtime story using the photographs as a stimulus for their own storytelling
	Independent work Ask the children to draw a picture of the story and write their narrative underneath. Remind them about use of informal and formal language.	
	Plenary Read the children a traditional folk story. Ask them to raise a hand if they hear an example of formal language and fold their arms for informal language.	

DAY 5 ◼ Formal language

Key features	Stages	Additional opportunities
	Introduction This session revises informal and formal language and looks at what motivates characters to feel and act the way they do. Re-read *Gran comes to visit parts 1* and *2* from the CD-ROM.	**Support:** sit the children in a circle and pass a toy around. Each child says one thing they know or feel about Gran
Communication: make connections and see relationships	**Speaking and listening** Sit the class in a circle. Ask for two volunteers to come to the middle, standing back to back, each holding a mobile phone (or miming holding mobile phones). One child will be in role as Gran. Ask members of the class to choose a situation for Gran where she needs to speak to someone on the phone (a friend, her daughter, the bank manager, the local MP). Once the situation is chosen, discuss whether the speech should be formal or informal. Ask the two volunteers to have a conversation as directed by the class.	**Extend:** give some children the challenge of reading stories of their own choice and identifying examples of formal and informal language
	Independent work Ask some children to write a letter as if they are Gran writing a formal letter to, for example, her bank in Australia telling them she is staying in England and would like some money transferred from her account to her daughter's account to pay for her share of the bills in the house. Ask other children to write as Gran texting, emailing or writing to a close friend telling them about her time in England.	
	Plenary Look together at some examples of the formal and informal writing. Discuss the differences.	

DAY 6 ◼ Clichés and expressions

Key features	Stages	Additional opportunities
	Introduction Talk about how, in stories, characters' talk varies depending on the age of the people. Phrases can be a good indicator of the age of the speaker. For example, older people may use different expressions from younger people, such as *bandy words* (1950s) rather than *had a row* (now).	
Communication: make connections and see relationships	**Speaking and listening** Look together at some examples of old fashioned expressions. Discuss some modern expressions used by people now. Challenge each pair to put together a short scene where one child is an older person using the old clichés and expressions speaking to a young person using their own clichés and expressions. This should be fun but might need a lot of your input.	**Support:** an adult might need to help 'draw out' the expression examples from some children
	Independent work Ask the children to draw a picture of the two characters and write some speech bubbles showing the difference in their speech.	**Extend:** a group could produce a class book of expressions to give the rest of the class some ideas for their writing
	Plenary Pin the drawings up on the wall. Let the children look around at them and discuss the different speech forms. Now invite some of the pairs to perform their conversation pieces from the speaking and listening activity.	

Guided reading

Find other stories from another culture. Discuss them as a group. Stop them at certain points and ask them to predict the next part of the story.

Invite them to create character sketches about some of the main characters.

Look for examples of informal and formal speech and, where possible, some examples of different use of language by different-aged people.

Assessment

Give children an extract from a favourite story. If possible it should contain two characters from different times and places. Ask them to complete the CD-ROM assessment activity sheet and share their answers with you. Can the children discuss how the characters' speech differs? Refer back to the learning outcomes on page 47.

Further work

Display an image taken in a different country, such as an African market scene, a tropical beach.

Invite the children to talk about the picture. Who might walk into the picture? Ask the children to close their eyes and think of a character. What would they be thinking? doing? feeling?

Challenge the children to write a story which features characters of different ages, showing the age difference by the way they speak.

Expressive language

■ Use the chart to write down examples of expressive language.

Story title: _____

Setting

Powerful verbs

Adjectives/adjectival phrases

PHOTOCOPIABLE  **SCHOLASTIC**
www.scholastic.co.uk

Figurative language

■ Find examples of the following language in your text.

Term	Definition	Example	My definition
Alliteration	The repetition of initial letter sounds in two or more neighbouring words or syllables.	The mad magic man made music.	
Cliché	An over familiar commonplace word or phrase.	Barking up the wrong tree.	
Hyperbole	Big exaggeration, usually with humour.	Mountains of work.	
Metaphor	Comparing two things by using one kind of object to suggest the likeness between them.	My memory is really foggy. There was a hail of bullets.	
Onomatopoeia	Naming a thing by imitating the sound associated with it.	Buzz, hiss, roar	
Personification	Give something human qualities.	The toy dog looked with a sad expression at the boy.	
Simile	A figure of speech comparing two unlike things that is often introduced by 'like' or 'as'.	As tall as a tree.	

NARRATIVE ■ UNIT 3

Asking questions

■ Use this chart to make notes about characters.

Character's name	Deductions from the text and the illustrations	What to find out	Question to ask

Name _____ Date _____

Paragraphs and apostrophes

■ Highlight where you think each paragraph should start. Add the apostrophes of omission and possession.

Pedro's New Friend
A story from Bolivia

In South America there is a tall range of mountains called the Andes. The air is thin and cold there and so people have to keep warm by wearing thick woollen capes called ponchos. On one of the mountains is a farm. It belongs to the family of a small boy called Pedro. Pedros family dont live at the farm. They have a house in the city but visit their farm once a year. One cold day Pedros father took him to visit their farm. They rode on horseback up the mountain. The farm dogs started barking. One dog was small and friendly. When Pedro called to it, the dog wagged its tail. When he jumped down from his horse the dog licked Pedros hand. "It looks like youve made a friend!" laughed Pedros father. It was cold on the farm and the farm workers gave Pedro a poncho to wear. All day the dog followed Pedro around. He started to get really fond of it. Later that day it started to get dark and Pedros father decided they should set off home. They mounted their horses and set off down the mountain. Pedros little friend, the dog, quietly followed his new friend all the way home!

Adaptation from 'Pedro's poncho' by Roger Hurn from *East of the sun, west of the moon* by Roger Hurn. Adaptation © 2007, Jay Mathews (2007, previously unpublished).

The day the sky was illuminated by a bonfire

■ Read the story and prepare an oral retelling.

In the Dreamtime there were no humans on Earth, only animals.

There was no sun, so everything was in darkness. Then two birds, the crane and the emu, had a fight.

They squabbled and argued for days and days. In the end, the crane took one of the emu's eggs from her nest and, with all her strength, hurled it into the air.

The egg hurtled past the clouds. Then, just when it seemed as if it would fly on up into the sky forever it hit a pile of firewood and smashed open. The egg yolk dripped onto the wood and set it alight. The fire blazed hot, and the huge flames lit up the world.

Down on Earth, the animals were amazed because the world was light. For the first time they could see.

A good spirit was watching over the animals. He could see how happy they were with the gift of sight and this gave him an idea.

With the help of his friends, the other spirits, he lit a bonfire every morning in the sky so that the animals on Earth would never again have to stumble around in the darkness.

Extract from *Bunda's dreamings* by Jay Mathews © 2006, Jay Mathews (2006, Literacy goes MADD).

PHOTOCOPIABLE   ■ **SCHOLASTIC**
www.scholastic.co.uk

NARRATIVE
UNIT 4 Stories which raise issues/dilemmas

Speak and listen for a range of purposes on paper and on screen

Strand 2 Listening and responding
■ Compare the different contributions of music, words and images in short extracts from TV programmes.
Strand 4 Drama
■ Create roles showing how behaviour can be interpreted from different viewpoints.

Read for a range of purposes on paper and on screen

Strand 7 Understanding and interpreting texts
■ Deduce characters' reasons for behaviour from their actions and explain how ideas are developed in non-fiction texts.
■ Explain how writers use figurative and expressive language to create images and atmosphere.

Write for a range of purposes on paper and on screen

Strand 9 Creating and shaping texts
■ Develop and refine ideas in writing using planning and problem-solving strategies.
■ Use settings and characterisation to engage readers' interest.
■ Show imagination through language used to create emphasis, humour, atmosphere or suspense.
■ Choose and combine words, images and other features for particular effects.
Strand 10 Text structure and organisation
■ Organise texts into paragraphs to distinguish between different information, events or processes.
Strand 11 Sentence structure and punctuation
■ Clarify meaning and point of view by using varied sentence structure (phrases, clauses and adverbials).
■ Use commas to mark clauses and the apostrophe for possession.

Progression in narrative

In this year children are moving towards:
■ Discussing the decisions that the author has made in setting up issues for the characters and choosing how to resolve them; commenting on the success of the writing and whether they agree or disagree with the way that problem was solved.
■ Looking at the way key characters respond to a dilemma and make deductions about their motives and feelings; exploring alternative outcomes to the main issue; analysing dialogue and making judgements about the extent to which characters reveal their true feelings and motives.
■ Using improvisation to explore alternative actions and outcomes to a particular issue.
■ Writing in role as a character from a story.
■ Planning and writing a longer story where the central character faces a dilemma; using a clear story structure organised into chapters; including character descriptions designed to provoke sympathy or dislike in the reader and using some figurative or expressive language to build detail.

UNIT 4 ◄ Stories which raise issues/dilemmas *continued*

Key aspects of learning covered in this Unit

Creative thinking
Children will ask why, how, what if or unusual questions. They will look and think about things differently and from other points of view.

Information processing
Children will summarise information.

Reasoning
Children will predict and anticipate events.

Empathy
Children will be encouraged to express their own views, opinions and preferences; take an interest in, watch and listen to other people; understand the perspective of another person; recognise and anticipate the thoughts and feelings of others in different situations, basing this on their own experience.

Social skills
Opportunities will be given for children to respond to others' views when they are different from their own.

Prior learning

Before starting this Unit check that the children can:
■ Understand how settings influence events and incidents in stories and how they affect characters' behaviour.
■ Understand the use of expressive and figurative language in prose.
If they need further support, please refer to a prior Unit or a similar Unit in Year 3.

Resources

Phase 1:
Benjy's ghost extracts 1 and *2* by Jacqueline Roy ✲; Digital camera; Well-known stories, including some with issues/dilemmas; Reading journals; Photocopiable page 77 'Story resolution plans'

Phase 2:
Old Dan and the stray dog by Jay Mathews ✲; Picture of a busy town scene; Musical instruments; A story with a moral issue or dilemma; Photocopiable page 78 'Dear Mr Mayor'

Phase 3:
When Jessie came across the sea Extracts 1–5 by Amy Hest ✲; A film of a journey; Digital camera and image-editing software; A story with an issue or dilemma; A novel or longer story; Photocopiable page 79 'Head or heart?'; Photocopiable page 80 'Why I should go to America'; Assessment activity 'Story endings' ✲

Cross-curricular opportunities

PSHE issues of loss, loneliness, old age and divorce
Journeys and travellers/settlers

UNIT 4 ■ Teaching sequence

Phase	Children's objectives	Summary of activities	Learning outcomes
1	I can identify issues and dilemmas in stories. I know how to use expressive language when I write a story. I can plan and write notes for a story resolution. I can write a story ending.	Identify key points and issues in a story. Freeze-frame ideas for resolving issues. Write using expressive language. Plan ideas for resolving problems. Write the final version of their resolutions.	Children can identify and summarise issues and how characters deal with them. Children can write critically about an issue. Children can write a story containing a dilemma.
2	I can find out about a character, develop a drama. I can understand the feelings of a character in a story. I can participate in a movement sequence exploring the character relationships. I understand different-length sentences create effects. I understand that certain words and phrases create different feelings in the reader. I can participate in a debate and offer ideas in role, to resolve a problem. I can write a letter in role.	Search a text for facts and inferences about the main character. Bring a scene alive considering the reactions of each character. Create a simple paired movement dance. Develop relevant adverbs, adjectives. Look at a piece of text and consider the effect of different-length sentences. Suggest what might have happened before and after the story incident. Debate as a class the issue of integration, using the story as a stimulus. Plan and write a persuasive letter.	Children can focus on a problem faced by a character. Children can identify and discuss evidence in the text that suggests characters' point of view and their possible actions. Children can create scenes in drama from the story and explore characters' thoughts and motives. Children can write in role as a character advising the main character about what they should do.
3	I can use freeze-frame and spotlighting. I can write a letter in role. I can use paragraphs, clauses and connectives. I can find common themes in stories about journeys. I can plan a story about an amazing journey. I can develop an effective story opening and create a character. I can add atmosphere and mood to a story. I can list climaxes and dilemmas from stories I know. I can identify story endings that have things in common. I can complete my own story. I can recognise and use connectives.	Find out about two characters using freeze-frame and spotlighting. Write letters in role as a character. Use paragraphs, clauses and connectives. Look at examples of adventure stories on DVD. Plan an adventure story. Develop characters through improvised drama then plan a first chapter. Plan and write chapter 2 of their story. Plan and write chapter 3 of their story. Look for exciting use of grammar. Develop good story endings. Look at connectives. Word-process stories.	Children can explore a setting, characters and issue or dilemma. Children can use this to plan a longer story arranged into chapters.

Provide copies of the objectives for the children.

DAY 1 ◼ Issues and dilemmas

Key features	Stages	Additional opportunities
Creative thinking: ask why, how, what if or unusual questions; look and think about things differently and from other points of view **Information processing:** summarise information	**Introduction** Read extract 1 of *Benjy's ghost* from the CD-ROM. Use different voices for the different characters to make it clear to the children how each character is feeling. Tell the children you want them to identify the issues and dilemmas raised in the story extract. Discuss what key issues are addressed in the story, for example his mother leaving home, his father marrying Benjy's detested teacher. Write the key issues on the board. **Speaking and listening** In small groups discuss Benjy's plight. Ask the children to think of some questions to ask Benjy and his father using the *wh* questioning words – who, why, what, where, when. Hot-seat yourself or a confident child as Benjy or his father and encourage the children to ask their *wh* questions. **Independent work** Hand out one copy of the text between two. Ask the pairs to find examples from the text showing Benjy's anxiety and some examples of how his father tried to reassure him. Does the author make effective use of figurative and expressive language to help the reader relate to the character's plight? **Plenary** Sit in a circle. Discuss the issues facing the characters in *Benjy's ghost*. These situations happen in real life. Can anyone relate to Benjy's dilemma? Can anyone think of some ideas to help Benjy come to terms with his problem?	**Storytelling:** a small group retell the story extract; encourage them to use expressive voices **Extend:** half the class walk around the room as Dad and the other half as Benjy; on command from you, they freeze and you spotlight some children to hear what the characters are thinking and feeling

DAY 2 ◼ Predictions

Key features	Stages	Additional opportunities
Reasoning: predict and anticipate events **Empathy:** express their own views, opinions and preferences; take an interest in, watch and listen to other people	**Introduction** Read *Benjy's ghost extract 1* again. Ask the children to predict what might happen in the story to resolve Benjy's issues and Dad's dilemmas. Write some of the predictions on the board. **Speaking and listening** Ask some pairs or small groups to come to the front and develop freeze-frame scenarios showing their ideas for resolving the characters' issues and dilemmas. Take digital pictures of their freeze-frame predictions. Ask the children to suggest captions for each freeze-frame. Invite the children doing the freeze-frames to 'come alive' and improvise the class's suggested predictions, such as *Dad promising that even though he is marrying Carol, he will spend time each week just with Benjy – giving him 'special' time.* **Independent work** Print out the photographs of the freeze-frames. Give pairs of children one each and ask them to write their own captions. They should stick their copy of their freeze-frame prediction on a piece of paper and write a description of their prediction. Encourage them to use expressive language and think about the power of varying the length of sentences. **Plenary** Encourage some children to read their captions and let the class give their opinions about them.	**Support:** what happens next? some children could mime an action and stop halfway through; the others have to guess want happens next

DAY 3 ■ Outcomes

Key features	Stages	Additional opportunities
	### Introduction In this session, the children are going to consider the possible courses of action suggested in the last session and 'bring them alive' in improvised drama scenes. Read some endings from well-known stories, which feature the resolution of issues. Can the children see any features common to story endings? Model how to write a good ending for a story, inviting the children to contribute.	**Dance:** create a simple movement sequence which shows: two people in harmony with each other (moving in sequence); a third person entering the scene and creating conflict; one person caught between the two other friends, trying to placate each and being pulled in two directions
Social skills: respond to others' views when they are different from their own **Empathy:** understand the perspective of another person	### Speaking and listening Divide the class in half, then into small groups within each half. One half takes the story prediction and develops an improvised scene from Dad's perspective and the other half develops an improvised scene from Benjy's perspective. ### Independent work Hand out photocopiable page 77 'Story resolution plans' and ask the children to write notes and draw sketches as a plan for their own resolutions. Encourage pairs to share their story resolution plans with each other. Ask them to comment on the effectiveness of their partner's ideas. ### Plenary Discuss how behaviour can be interpreted from different viewpoints: Dad and Benjy both misunderstand each other's behaviour. Now discuss the alternative resolution ideas. Which ending do the children prefer? Why?	

DAY 4 ■ Resolving issues

Key features	Stages	Additional opportunities
	### Introduction Children are going to take their plans and write them as a resolution of the dilemmas and issues facing the characters in *Benjy's ghost*. Talk about the use of persuasive language, for example how Dad convinces Benjy that everything will be alright.	
Empathy: recognise and anticipate the thoughts and feelings of others in different situations, basing this on their own experience	### Speaking and listening Ask a child to come and act as Benjy while you play the part of Dad. Tell the children they can help resolve Benjy and his father's dilemmas by suggesting what each might say to each other and how the action should develop. You and the child volunteer should wait until someone suggests an opening speech then interpret that in action. Stop and wait for the next suggestion from the class then act that bit. Continue until the scene is completed. Demonstrate how to turn this improvisation into a written story ending on the board. Focus on the effective use of persuasive language. ### Independent work Ask the children to revisit their story resolution plans and develop them into the final paragraphs of the story extract. ### Plenary Read *Benjy's ghost extract 2* from the CD-ROM. They need to know that this is not the end of the whole novel, just the resolution of the incident in chapter 3 of the story. Did anyone develop the same resolution in his or her version?	**Discussion:** hold a circle time discussion where the children relate to Benjy's situation and think of some ideas to help comfort him or help him resolve his problems

Guided reading and writing

Read the extracts from *Benjy's ghost* as a group.

Discuss the issues which exist between the main characters and the dilemmas these relationships cause.

Write a letter to Benjy, Dad or Carol giving them some advice about how to deal with the difficult situation the character finds him/herself in.

Assessment

Read another story to the children in which the characters have issues or face dilemmas.

Ask them to: identify the main key points from the story; write the key points in sentences; work out in an improvised drama how to resolve the issues being faced by the characters. Make a note of each child's response. Refer back to the learning outcomes on page 65.

Further work

Ask the children to find stories which have issues and dilemmas.

Ask them to read their chosen story then to write a review of the story in their reading journals.

They should try to summarise the story and then give their opinion of the plot.

DAY 1 ■ Facts and inferences

Key features	Stages	Additional opportunities
	### Introduction Read *Old Dan and the stray dog parts 1* and *2* from the CD-ROM, where he is in the town waiting to cross the road. Ask the children to search the text for facts about Old Dan. What inferences can they make about him? Can they explain their inferences?	
Social skills: respond to others' views when they are different from their own	### Speaking and listening In groups discuss who might be in the town and what they would be doing, where they might be going, what they might be thinking or feeling. (Find a good illustration of a busy town scene to display to give them some ideas.) Ask each child to pick a character and create a frozen picture. 'Bring the scene alive.' At your signal, everyone freezes again, and you spotlight a group at a time to hear what they are thinking and saying. Each character should have one line to say.	**Music:** give a group some instruments and ask them to create their own town soundscape
Empathy: understand the perspective of another person	### Independent work Children should complete a character sketch about their chosen character by drawing him/her and writing a description underneath and a speech bubble filled with their 'one liner' speech from the freeze-frame activity	
	### Plenary Sit in a circle and ask each child to introduce him/herself in role.	

DAY 2 ■ Exploring issues and dilemmas

Key features	Stages	Additional opportunities
Creative thinking: ask why, how, what if or unusual questions	### Introduction Recap on Day 1's activities. Ask the children to get back in role as their chosen character from the town scene. Discuss how each character might feel about Old Dan, perhaps scared of him, annoyed with his brusque attitude, totally uncaring about him. What would their character actually say about him when he arrived in the town?	**Support:** some children could draw a picture showing how their particular character might feel
	### Speaking and listening Set up the town scene again. Invite a confident child to don a role-play hat or coat and send him/her through the 'town' as Old Dan. As he approaches each group, they come alive and, in role as their character, say out loud what they think or feel about Old Dan. Ask them to be either indifferent, uncaring or unpleasant towards him. Ask Old Dan to take off his role-play hat/coat and tell the class how he felt when the townsfolk spoke their thoughts about him.	**Extend:** a group could plan, perform and film their scene to show to the rest of the class
	### Independent work Write Old Dan's thoughts in speech bubbles on the board. Ask each child to write their speech on big cut-out speech bubbles.	
	### Plenary Invite the class to hot-seat you (or a confident child) as Old Dan to find out more about him.	

DAY 3 ▮ The stray dog

Key features	Stages	Additional opportunities
Social skills: respond to others' views when they are different from their own	**Introduction** Read *Old Dan and the stray dog parts 1* and *2* from the CD-ROM, where he meets the dog. Talk about the message in this part of the extract, for example unhappy dog, angry old man. Ask the children to point out parts of the text which give the reader a clear picture about the underlying emotions and feelings.	
	Speaking and listening In pairs, ask the children to create a simple paired movement sequence showing the nervous, cowering dog and the gentle persuasive man. Watch some of the dances. Ask the children to give you some descriptive words and phrases from their dance movements. Write them on the board. Can the children identify what these words and phases are, for example adjectives, adverbs, verbs?	**Support:** some children will need an adult to scribe their writing
Empathy: understand the perspective of another person	**Independent work** Ask the children to write words, phrases and examples of figurative and expressive language as inspired by their dance. Now ask each child to create a short descriptive paragraph entitled, 'The stray dog.' Encourage them to describe their own feelings about the dog's plight.	**Extend:** research and present a short talk to the class about the RSPCA; there could be a discussion about issues of cruelty to animals
	Plenary Read some of the descriptive paragraphs. Discuss the way the writers have expressed their emotions using figurative and expressive language.	

DAY 4 ▮ How I look and how I feel

Key features	Stages	Additional opportunities
	Introduction Read the end of the of the story where Old Dan says, *Let's get you back to my house. Then we can decide what to do for the best.* Why is *we* important? Old Dan thinks the people are interfering and he wants to make the decision about the future of the dog. Write the children's thoughts on the board.	
	Speaking and listening Read the part of the story where the crowd gathers and everyone has some idea and suggestion to make. Can the children see the differences in length of the sentences? There are longer sentences for the descriptions, shorter sentences for the townspeople's comments. What effect does this create?	**Role play:** recreate the scene between Dan and the people in the crowd; work on body language
Empathy: recognise and anticipate the thoughts and feelings of others in different situations, basing this on their own experience	**Independent work** Discuss Old Dan's reasons for wanting to take the dog home, for example reminds him of himself, would be like a replacement for Sammy, hated the way the dog had been abandoned by its owners. Ask questions to see if the children understand the way Old Dan was actually feeling as opposed to how other people thought he was feeling. Why did Old Dan smile as he walked away from the crowd? How do we know the way he felt?	
	Plenary Display the text. Invite the children to pick out effective language.	

DAY 5 ■ What happened next

Key features	Stages	Additional opportunities
Empathy: recognise and anticipate the thoughts and feelings of others in different situations, basing this on their own experience	**Introduction** Ask the children some questions to find out their understanding of the underlying emotions *Old Dan and the stray dog*. What had happened to the dog in the past? What emotions did the children feel when reading the part of the story where the dog first began to trust Old Dan. Which phrases/words used by the author actually create these emotions in the reader? Discuss cruelty to animals. Why do they think the dog's owners abandoned him?	
Reasoning: predict and anticipate events	**Speaking and listening** Ask the children, in pairs, to predict what might happen next in the story. Challenge them to create a simple role play from their ideas. Then collect children's words and phrases describing their 'what happened next' ideas.	**Music:** compose musical representations of 'what happened next,' showing the contrast of mood between the two new friends
	Independent work Give each pair of children a piece of paper and ask them to write their 'what happened next' scene in the form of a cartoon strip, drawing their pictures and, writing either speech bubbles on each illustration or short pieces of text in the text boxes underneath each picture.	
	Plenary Swap the cartoon strips around and ask the children to dramatise someone else's ideas for 'what happened next'. Invite some groups to perform their new scenes. Encourage comments and suggestions for improvement.	

DAY 6 ■ Problem solving

Key features	Stages	Additional opportunities
	Introduction Display *Old Dan and the stray dog*. What do the children notice about the relationship between the man and the dog, for example in the scene *He looked at the man. The man looked steadily back at him*? At the end of the story, Old Dan smiles. What is the significance of him smiling? Notice how short but powerful the last sentence is.	**Support:** plan the groupings for the role-play carefully to give support to the children who need it
Social skills: respond to others' views when they are different from their own	**Speaking and listening** Remind children about the characters they created for the town scene on Days 1 and 2 of this Phase. Ask them to regroup as their characters and be gossiping and chatting about Old Dan having taken the stray dog back to his home. Call the group (in role) together for a town council meeting. In role as the mayor read them the letter from Old Dan to the townsfolk on photocopiable page 78. Lead a lively debate with the townspeople giving their thoughts about how Dan could be come a central figure in the town.	**Extend:** a confident child could take the role of the mayor or a group of capable children could be a committee or council
	Independent work Divide the class into small groups and ask them to think of ideas and practical suggestions. Each group could have a scribe and a spokesperson.	
	Plenary Bring the class back together and listen to the points of view. Decide on a course of action. A vote may be needed if there is more than one idea.	

DAY 7 ■ Dear Dan

Key features	Stages	Additional opportunities

Stages

Introduction
In this session, the children are going to write letters to Dan in role as their characters from the town. Model a letter on the board. Paragraph 1 should be a response to Old Dan's letter, paragraph 2 their own individual response to the sentiments of his letter including an honest appraisal of their own response to Old Dan and maybe an apology for any misunderstandings. Paragraph 3 should be suggestions and an invitation to Old Dan. Try to make a light-hearted or amusing comment to lighten the mood and extend an 'olive branch' to Dan.

Speaking and listening
Give pairs of children extracts from the text. Ask them to look for use of possessive apostrophes and commas in the text to remind them how to use these in their own writing.

Independent work
Ask each child to write to Dan, in role as their character, telling him his/her thoughts and feelings about the past and suggesting a way forward. They should use the three-paragraph model demonstrated in the introduction.

Plenary
Invite a child to act as Dan and attend a meeting of the townsfolk. Stand the children in a circle. Dan stands in the middle. He can then point to any of the 'townsfolk' and they will offer him supportive ideas and suggestions to help him become a member of the community again.

Key features

Empathy: express their own views, opinions and preferences

Additional opportunities

Art: draw a series of pictures showing Old Dan after he has become a friend of the town; what is he doing? What is he thinking? How is he feeling?

Guided writing
Tell the class that setting up a moral dilemma is a good way to start a story. Model how to do this, for example *Steven was on his way out to play when he saw Maxine slip back into the classroom. He followed her and peeped in through the door. Maxine had her hand inside the teacher's coat. Steven turned and hurried away before Maxine saw him. He didn't know what to do. Should he tell the teacher or should he say nothing?* Discuss Steven's options. Both will have consequences. What will these consequences be? Children write their own choice of ending.

Assessment
Give children a story with moral dilemmas or issues.
Ask them questions, for example: What is the main issue facing the main character? How does the author describe the issue? How would you resolve the issue? What use does the author make of a combination of short and long clauses?
Refer back to the learning outcomes on page 65.

Further work
Children could devise a questionnaire or interview other children to find out how they would react if they had a certain moral issue or dilemma to deal with.

DAY 1 ■ Heart or head

Key features	Stages	Additional opportunities
Empathy: express their own views, opinions and preferences	### Introduction Read the extracts *When Jessie came across the sea* from the CD-ROM. Find facts and inferences about Granny and Jessie. Discuss the setting of the story. From this the children will deduce their home is isolated, they are very poor and Jessie might have a better life in America but also that they are very close and would miss each other. How would the children in the class feel about leaving home to go to live in another country?	
Creative thinking: ask why, how, what if or unusual questions	### Speaking and listening Prepare questions for Jessie and Granny. Hot-seat confident children (or yourself) as the characters to find out more about their lives, their past, their hopes and dreams for the future. In circle time, ask the children to tell you what they now know about the characters. Pairs should then create a freeze-frame where Jessie and Granny have received the news about Jessie's opportunity. Each child thinks of one thought and one speech. Thoughts will be different from speech. Talk about how we often think one thing but say another. Why is this?	**Support:** give children a cut-out thought bubble and a cut-out speech bubble to write or draw their thoughts and their actual speech; stick them on the wall under headings *Thoughts* and *Speech*
	### Independent work Give each child photocopiable page 79 'Head or heart?' and ask them to complete the images of Granny and Jessie and complete the speech and thought bubbles.	**Extend:** write a short diary entry as if they are granny; express her innermost thoughts and emotions
	### Plenary Watch some of the role plays and read some of the children's writing. Discuss what makes them effective.	

DAY 2 ■ Why I should go to America

Key features	Stages	Additional opportunities
	### Introduction Re-read the extracts *When Jessie came across the sea* from the CD-ROM. Focus on the part where the rabbi tells the villagers about the ticket to America and each villager tries to persuade him they should be the one to go.	
Empathy: understand the perspective of another person	### Speaking and listening Role play a scene where the class become characters in the village and have their own ideas about why they would be the best person to have the ticket to America. Spend some time discussing the kind of activities and jobs which villagers would need to do in such an isolated and primitive rural setting.	**Support:** create a postcard to the rabbi with a picture on one side and the writing on the other
	### Independent work Ask children, in role as a village character, to write a letter to the rabbi to tell him their reasons for being the best person to have the ticket. Give them photocopiable page 80 'Why I should go to America' to help them with their planning. Discuss how they should make their letters interesting. Each villager has to 'sell' themselves, their personality and their skills to try to impress the rabbi. Discuss how to start the letter, what to include and in what order.	**Extend:** a group could produce short video sequences of themselves in role as the characters telling the rabbi about themselves
	### Plenary In role as the rabbi, create the scene where the villagers come to the rabbi's house in the night to tell him why they should go. Listen to their pleas and comment on the effectiveness of their persuasive arguments.	

DAY 3 ◼ Effective use of grammar

Key features	Stages	Additional opportunities
	Introduction Revisit the letters written by the 'villagers' to the rabbi in the last session. Choose one to model on the board. Ask the class to look carefully at it, comment on any examples of good use of paragraphs, clauses, connectives, conjunctions, adverbial and powerful verbs.	**Role play:** in pairs, invite one to 'sell' the other by interviewing them in role as the villager to find out more about them then, together, designing a poster with annotations and slogans to 'sell' the person to the rabbi as the best person to go to America
	Speaking and listening Invite the class to help you further enhance the letter by adding some of the above grammar skills, for example *I am a carpenter. I make tables and chairs for the villagers – I am a skilled carpenter who fashions stylish tables in addition to graceful, strong chairs for discerning customers.*	
Empathy: understand the perspective of another person	**Independent work** In pairs ask the children to discuss if and how the embellishments have enhanced the reader's understanding of the skills of the carpenter. Devise some grammar exercises for the children, using the text *When Jessie came across the sea* as a stimulus.	
	Plenary Display the exercises. Invite children to come to the front and help you to complete the answers to the questions. Discuss how there isn't one right answer to some of the questions; they are open to allow the children to be creative in their responses.	

DAY 4 ◼ The amazing journey

Key features	Stages	Additional opportunities
	Introduction Remind the class that Jessie was going on a long journey to America at the turn of the 19th century. Discuss the dangers she might have faced on the long voyage across the sea and when she arrived in America. If possible, get a copy of the book and read the whole story to the children.	**Authors:** invite an author to speak to the class about writing a longer novel in chapters; the class should, if possible, have read some of the author's books and have prepared some questions to ask
Information processing: summarise information	**Speaking and listening** Show children a film showing characters making a journey (copyright permitting). Discuss common features in stories about journeys, for example a growing-up process, a determination to get to the end for a specific purpose, meeting danger on the way, finding inner strengths and bravery, bonding with other/new characters.	
	Independent work Tell the children that they are going to be planning and writing their own adventure journey stories in pairs. They will be in chapters but will still use a story-planning skeleton or story mountain. Give them time to think about and plan a story skeleton. The story should involve two main characters on an amazing journey and have a beginning, build-up, climax/dilemma and a resolution.	**Extend:** some children could write notes as the author is talking
	Plenary Share some of the children's ideas. Ask the class to add their own ideas and suggestions to help the authors develop their ideas further.	

DAY 5 ■ Developing our stories

Key features	Stages	Additional opportunities
Empathy: recognise and anticipate the thoughts and feelings of others in different situations	**Introduction** Model how to write an effective opening to a story. Explain to the children that they are going to 'flesh out' their main characters through improvised drama showing their characters in the beginning of their story. **Speaking and listening** Pairs plan their improvisation: Where? When? What? Why? Encourage them to think about the characters' personalities and how they interact. Are they friends, enemies, relatives, strangers? Watch some of the character scenarios. Model on the board how to capture the key points. **Independent work/Plenary** Let children sketch their characters and then write their first story chapter based on their ideas in the improvisations.	**Support:** provide a storyboard to help develop the first chapter of their story in four stages/paragraphs **Extend:** some children could move forward and continue writing their story chapters on their own

DAY 6 ■ The adventure starts

Key features	Stages	Additional opportunities
Creative thinking: look and think about things differently and from other points of view	**Introduction** Remind the class about how the setting and atmosphere influence the moods and actions of the characters in stories. Read some examples together. **Speaking and listening** Let pairs revisit their story planning and discuss the contents of chapter 2 – the build-up. Ask them to sketch their settings and write words and phrases around the edge. They should now develop an oral storytelling of the second chapter of their story to present to the rest of the class. Encourage them to use exciting language, adjectival phrases and powerful verbs when describing the setting. **Independent work/Plenary** Organise the pairs to perform their oral storytellings. Encourage the class to make positive comments and give ideas for improvement.	**Support:** give children some images of settings. Ask them to describe how they feel when they look at the pictures **Extend:** take digital pictures of settings and use photograph-editing programmes

DAY 7 ■ The story climax/dilemma

Key features	Stages	Additional opportunities
Creative thinking: look and think about things differently and from other points of view	**Introduction** Read some of the children's stories so far. Identify examples of effective grammar, paragraphs, commas, adjectives, powerful verbs. **Speaking and listening** Ask the class to compile a list of story climaxes/dilemmas from stories they have read and from their own story planning. Ask them to write some of their ideas on sticky notes placed onto a wall of story climax/dilemma ideas. **Independent work** Encourage the children to write the climax/dilemma chapter of their story. **Plenary** Ask some children to read their chapters. Note the use of effective grammar.	**Support:** focus on one aspect of grammar at a time **Extend:** produce an effective grammar poster to help other children learn

DAY 8 ▪ Story endings

Key features	Stages	Additional opportunities
	Introduction Read some story endings to the class. Ask them to identify some common features of story endings. Model a story ending on the board, encouraging the children to help you. Check that they are confident about using direct speech in their story writing. Ask them to read the Jessie extracts again and pick out some direct speech, commas and speech marks. Ask the children to check their own stories for speech and correct use of speech marks.	**Support:** give a group some cards with direct speech on them; encourage them to read the speech out loud using expressive voices
	Speaking and listening Ask the pairs of children to prepare a drama improvisation of their own story ending. They could start in a freeze-frame, come alive to perform their story ending then finish in another freeze-frame position.	
	Independent work Children write their ending chapter. Remind them about the impact of using varied sentence length to create impact in their story writing.	**Extend:** ask some children to look at examples of book reviews in newspapers and magazines; Can they write a critique on their own story?
Empathy: express own views, opinions and preferences	**Plenary** Let the children read their stories in groups and comment on each other's work.	

DAY 9 ▪ Connectives and debates

Key features	Stages	Additional opportunities
	Introduction Display a piece of text on the board. Invite children to come out and underline connectives (adverbs, adverbial phrases, conjunctions).	**Support:** provide individual or group support
Empathy: express own views, opinions and preferences	**Speaking and listening** Hold a debate about a current issue relevant to your class. Encourage the children to use some of the connectives from the passage above.	**Extend:** a group could take their story books to the local library and read them to a younger group of children
	Independent work Give children time to complete their stories by word-processing, illustrating, book making.	
	Plenary Ask children to read their stories to children in another class.	

Guided writing
Read a story with an issue or dilemma. Stop at a point before the dilemma is resolved. Can the class identify the dilemma? What would they do in the situation?
Ask the children to write a persuasive argument using connectives.

Assessment
Give the children the CD-ROM assessment sheet. Ask them to read the story and summarise the key points. Hold a discussion about the dilemma. Can they write their own alternative endings?
Refer back to the learning outcomes on page 65.

Further work
Read a longer story or novel with the class. Ask them to read it as if they are reviewing it for a local newspaper. Hold a discussion with the children. Ask them to give their viewpoints and back them up with examples from the story.

Story resolution plans

■ Use the chart below to plan your own resolution.

Story ending from the perspective of Benjy/Benjy's Dad. (cross out one or the other)
My story ending sketch:
Part 1 of my story ending:
Part 2 of my story ending:

Dark House,

High Hill,

Townsville

Dear Mr Mayor and friends,

You will be aware that for many years I have been living on my own in my house on the hill. I rarely come down to the town and when I do it is only because I need to go to the supermarket or change my books at the library.

Part of the reason I don't like coming to town is because I know what you all think of me. You don't think I hear you when you call me 'miserable anti-social old man,' or when the children rush past my house screaming, "The scary old man's going to get me."

Well I do hear you, and it hurts my feelings. When I do come to town every one is busy rushing about and everyone ignores me. That's why I don't look at anyone or speak to anyone.

Anyway, something amazing happened last week. I expect you've all heard that I found a stray dog when I was in the town and took him home with me to decide what to do. I want you to know that I have checked with the RSPCA and the local vets. They told me that the dog was micro chipped. They looked their records and then traced his owners. That lady in the town was right when she said they'd left the dog behind when they moved away from the town. They don't want him any more. When I said I'd like to keep him, they were more than happy to let me have him.

The dog is called Louie. He is really gentle and friendly and very well trained. I want you all to know that, since he has come to live with me, I feel differently about life. I have a new friend to look after, take for walks and share things with. Because I'm feeling so much better, it got me thinking that maybe its time for me to start afresh.

I'm sorry for the way I've behaved over the years and would like to find a way to become a part of the town community again, the way I was before my wife died.

So I'm writing to you to ask you if you could think of a way you could help me to achieve this. I have a few ideas of my own but I think it would be better if you all tell me your ideas.

I hope you will think seriously about my request.

I am your sincerely,

Dan Boyd.

Dan Boyd

Text © 2007, Jay Mathews (2007, previously unpublished).

Head or heart?

 Complete the pictures of Granny and Jessie and write one thing they are thinking and one thing they are saying.

Illustration © Nova Developments.

Why I should go to America

■ Draw a picture of your character (one of the villagers). Fill the boxes with reasons why you should go to America. Be as confident a character as possible.

Why I should go to America.

Reason 1:

Why I should go to America.

Reason 2:

Why I should go to America.

Reason 3:

■ 100 LITERACY FRAMEWORK LESSONS YEAR 4

PHOTOCOPIABLE
www.scholastic.co.uk

NARRATIVE
UNIT 5 Plays

Speak and listen for a range of purposes on paper and on screen

Strand 1 Speaking
- Use and reflect on some ground rules for sustaining talk and interactions.

Strand 4 Drama
- Create roles showing how behaviour can be interpreted from different viewpoints.
- Develop scripts based on improvisation.
- Comment constructively on plays and performances, discussing effects and how they are achieved.

Read for a range of purposes on paper and on screen

Strand 7 Understanding and interpreting texts
- Deduce characters' reasons for behaviour from their actions and explain how ideas are developed in non-fiction texts.
- Explain how writers use figurative and expressive language to create images and atmosphere.

Write for a range of purposes on paper and on screen

Strand 9 Creating and shaping texts
- Develop and refine ideas in writing using planning and problem-solving strategies.
- Show imagination through language used to create emphasis, humour, atmosphere or suspense.
- Choose and combine words, images and other features for particular effects.

Strand 11 Sentence structure and punctuation
- Clarify meaning and point of view by using varied sentence structure (phrases, clauses and adverbials).

Strand 12 Presentation
- Write consistently with neat, legible and joined handwriting.

Progression in narrative

In this year children are moving towards:
- Looking for the way characters behave in different settings.
- Writing and resolving dilemmas.
- Planning complete stories (playscripts) by identifying the stages in a story.
- Exploring the relationships between characters.
- Using details to build character descriptions and evoke a response from the readers.
- Understanding the conventions of reading, writing and performing playscripts.

UNIT 5 ◄ **Plays** *continued*

Key aspects of learning covered in this Unit

Enquiry
Children will need to draw conclusions and evaluate outcomes.

Creative thinking
Children will generate imaginative ideas in response to stimuli. They will discover and make connections through play and experimentation. They will be encouraged to look at and think about things differently and from other points of view. They should apply imaginative thinking to achieve an objective and reflect critically on ideas, actions and outcomes.

Information processing
Children will record information using a given format and using formats they have devised.

Reasoning
Children will predict and anticipate events. They should use the language of sequence.

Evaluation
Children will be encouraged to express their own views , opinions and preferences and evaluate the quality of an outcome.

Prior learning

Before starting this Unit check that the children can:
■ Read, prepare and present playscripts.
■ Recognise the key differences between prose and playscript, for example by looking at dialogue, stage directions, layout of text.
If they need further support please refer to a prior Unit or a similar Unit in Year 3.

Resources

Phase 1:
Just like us by Bill Tordoff ✖; A play on DVD or video; short playscripts; Percussion instruments and/or music software (optional); A story extract with lots of dialogue; Digital camera; Photocopiable page 94 'Playscripts'; Photocopiable page 95 'Stage directions'

Phase 2:
Soft toys and puppets; Children's puppetry/animation on DVD or video; Digital still and video cameras; Tape recorder; Photocopiable page 96 'Storyboard'

Phase 3:
Character, setting and dilemma cards (see Day 1); *Granny I'm home!* by Jay Mathews ✖; Nursery rhymes; Playscript stimulus such as a story or image; Story props; Playscripts; Photographs of different people; Assessment activity 'Playscript' ✖

Cross-curricular opportunities

History project about the Second World War, particularly evacuees
PSHE (SEAL): people aren't always what they seem
RE study of creation stories from other cultures

UNIT 5 ■ Teaching sequence

Phase	Children's objectives	Summary of activities	Learning outcomes
1	I can recognise a playscript and know how to use one. I understand why a playscript needs stage directions. I can participate in an improvisation for a new scene in a play. I can identify the effects created by music and sound effects in a play. I can create a simple playscript from a well-known story. I can use language imaginatively to create emphasis, humour, atmosphere or suspense.	Look at playscript conventions. Improvise short play scenarios. Look at stage directions. Read a script and respond to stage directions but also use own initiative. Improvise a new scene for the characters in *Just like us* and write a character sketch. Look at examples of films and plays on DVD or video. Discuss the effects of music and sound effects. Turn well-known stories into playscripts. Predict what happens next in a playscript and improvise the scenes.	Children know the conventions of plays and the skills of improvised drama. Children can use stage directions within a playscript. Children can consider the effectiveness of their own and others' performances. Children can explore characters' characteristics, motives and relationships with others. Children can comment constructively on a professional performance. Children can create a simple planning storyboard with stage directions and suggestions for sound effects. Children can create a playscript of their own using script conventions, special effects and stage directions. Children can use imagination through language to create a 'what happened next' improvisation.
2	I can work with others to devise and plan a simple puppet play. I can analyse some aspects of plays and programmes for younger children and include them in my own puppet play. I can perform a puppet play with others in my group and listen to comments from the audience afterwards.	Devise simple puppet plays and develop oral scripts. Watch programmes for younger children and analyse them. Adjust own plays to meet the needs of a younger audience. Perform puppet plays to a younger audience. Listen to their views and comments. Write part of their scripts.	Children can work in a group discussing and planning the framework for a puppet play for a younger audience. Children can identify some key features of programmes for younger children and adapt their plays to suit the audience. Children can perform a puppet play to a younger audience and consider their responses.
3	I can work in a group developing an improvised scene using playscript cards. I can take part in both an improvised scene and a scripted scene. I can make decisions about the genre and plot for a new playscript. I can develop main characters for my playscript. I can use adverbs in stage directions. I can write the climax and resolution of my own play.	Engage in character, setting and dilemma activities. Devise a dialogue and record it as a playscript. Read a play extract about Granny and Bunda. Consider the advantages and disadvantages of using a playscript versus improvised drama. Project voices. Decide on the genre and plot of own playscripts. Develop characters for own plays. Use adverbs effectively in stage directions. Write opening scenes for own plays. Complete own playscripts. Agree criteria for choosing three scripts to use in performance.	Children can prepare and write a short play scene from character, settings and dilemmas provided by the teacher. Children can develop a play scene from a script and by improvisation. Children can plan their own playscripts. Children can develop and create characters for a playscript. Children can understand and recognise the effective use of adverbs in stage directions to guide actors. Children can complete a playscript. Children can consider how to create a climax and resolution in a story.

Provide copies of the objectives for the children.

DAY 1 ■ Playscripts

Key features	Stages	Additional opportunities
Creative thinking: generate imaginative ideas in response to stimuli	### Introduction Look together at the play extract *Just like us* by Bill Tordoff from the CD-ROM. Ask the children if they can explain what this is (a playscript). Elicit that plays are stories written for a performance. Discuss why it is written in this way, for example to give actors things to say, to give production teams prompts about what to do. Devise a list of playscript conventions with the class, for example *a list of characters; play divided into acts and scenes; stage directions (exits/entrances); directions for actors; no speech marks; every speech has a new line; character's name shown before the character's speech.*	
	### Speaking and listening In pairs, ask the children to devise an improvised scene about an everyday event, such as 'a surprise present', or 'The day Gran came to visit'.	**Support:** provide support; record their improvisation on a tape recorder or video
Information processing: record information using a given format	### Independent work Ask the pairs to have a go at writing the beginning of their scene as a playscript using photocopiable page 94 'Playscripts' as a guide.	**Extend:** write their whole scene rather than just the beginning part
	### Plenary View some of their improvised scenes. Invite the class to be an 'audience' and to make positive comments and suggestions for improvements. Some children might like to share their playscript planning with the class.	

DAY 2 ■ Stage directions

Key features	Stages	Additional opportunities
	### Introduction Look together at the stage directions for the actors within the play script *Just like us*, for example *Class start talking, The siren becomes audible again.* Ask the children why they think there is a need for these directions in a playscript.	
Evaluation: express their own views, opinions and preference	### Speaking and listening Give pairs of children the stage direction cards on photocopiable page 95 'Stage directions' and invite one child to read a stage direction and the other to act it out. Change around for the second direction and continue in this way until all directions have been tried out. Draw the class back together and watch a few performances. Comment on their effectiveness. Discuss how useful these would be if you were an actor trying to learn a part for a play.	**Support:** provide adult support to read out the stage direction cards
	### Independent work Organise the class into groups with a director in each group. Give each child a playscript of *Just like us* and ask the director to cast the scene and then hold a play reading. Encourage the children to bring their characters alive by use of vocal expression, facial expression and body language – responding to the stage directions but also using their own initiative and feelings.	**Extend:** challenge a group to write their own stage directions cards for others to try out
	### Plenary Listen to the play readings. Are the children only reading the speech? are they using good vocal expression and characterisation?	

DAY 3 ⬛ A new scene

Key features	Stages	Additional opportunities
	### Introduction Look again together at the playscript, *Just like us*. Remind the class about their play readings from Day 1. Do they feel they know their character better having 'brought them to life'? Ask them to suggest the characteristics of the main characters in the play extract from clues in the script, for example Character's name: *Michael*; Personality: *Lively, loud, good sense of humour*; Characteristics: *Always joking about and getting into trouble with the teacher.* Repeat this exercise with information about Bernard. Model the characterisations on the board.	**Support:** make a simple game of 'families'; each child invents a family, drawing each member onto a small bit of card and giving them names; put everyone's cards together, shuffle them and play the game (each child collects family members, the winner is the one with a complete family)
Creative thinking: discover and make connections through play and experimentation	### Speaking and listening Challenge the class, in small groups, to discuss a new improvised story scene which might be based on the original. It should show an insight into the life of either Bernard or Michael.	
	### Independent work Children should now write a description of either Bernard or Michael They should think about describing physical appearance, their behaviour, their nature, their relationship to other people in their family, their situation and how all this affects them emotionally.	**Extend:** film their scene
	### Plenary Discuss the children's ideas for their new scene. Invite some children to come to the front to read their descriptions and talk about their scene ideas.	

DAY 4 ⬛ Script writing

Key features	Stages	Additional opportunities
Creative thinking: reflect critically on ideas, actions and outcomes	### Introduction Watch an example of a play on DVD or video (copyright permitting). Talk with the class about what made it effective, for example actors knowing their lines; good acting techniques; where the actors stand, enter and exit; the use of music and sound effects to enhance the mood or atmosphere.	
	### Speaking and listening Read extracts from some other playscripts with the class. Invite some children to play the parts in the script whilst the rest read along. One person could read out the stage and acting directions in between the speeches.	**Support:** an adult could help a group by reading the stage and acting directions for them
Creative thinking: apply imaginative thinking to achieve an objective	### Independent work In pairs, re-read the play extract *Just like us*. Using a simple storyboard, ask them to sketch four parts of the scene in sequence and make notes about where they would use stage directions and effects, for example sound effects of air raid sirens, children's laughter and playground sounds, marching music for the exit.	**Extend:** create their own sound effects by using found sounds or percussion instruments or making sound effects on the computer
	### Plenary Let each pair swap their storyboard with another pair. Challenge them to create the play scene using just the directions on the storyboards. Ask some groups to present their scenes, and invite the original creators to comment on their interpretation.	

DAY 5 ▪ Text to script

Key features	Stages	Additional opportunities
Creative thinking: look at and think about things differently and from other points of view **Information processing:** record information using a given format	**Introduction** Talk about novels that have been turned into plays and films, such as *Lord of the Rings* and the *Harry Potter* stories. Tell the children you are going to demonstrate how to turn text into a playscript. Take one of the children's storyboards and demonstrate the conventions of script writing, including *stage directions, the name of the character who is about to speak followed by a colon (:) then what the character is going to say.* **Speaking and listening** Give each child a piece of story text which has plenty of speech in it and which is well known to the children. Ask them, in small groups, to improvise the story. **Independent work** Invite them, in pairs, to transform the story into a playscript using the conventions discussed in previous sessions and established above. Give an example such as *Mary ran out of the house yelling excitedly 'It's snowing!'* As a playscript this could be: *Stage directions – Mary runs out of the house. Mary: (shouting excitedly) It's snowing.* **Plenary** Read through some of the 'transferences'. Read the original text yourself and invite one of the children to read their playscript version. Encourage the children to use dynamic voices.	**Support:** an adult could undertake this activity with a group on the flipchart **Extend:** give a group a short piece of text which includes speech and ask them to transfer it into a playscript

DAY 6 ▪ What happened next?

Key features	Stages	Additional opportunities
Reasoning: predict and anticipate events; use the language of sequence **Information processing:** record information using formats they have devised **Evaluation:** evaluate the quality of an outcome	**Introduction** Read the play extract *Just like us* again. Ask the children to predict what might happen next in the story. Ask groups to show their scenes in freeze-frame drama. Take some digital images of them to use in the support activity. **Speaking and listening** Ask small groups to prepare an improvisation of their predicted 'what happens next' scenarios. Draw the class together and invite a few groups to perform their scenes. Ask the audience to make comments and suggestions for improvement. **Independent work** Ask the groups to record their 'what happened next' scenario onto a story skeleton planner, which they devise themselves, using ideas from the various models used in this and previous Units. **Plenary** Ask the support group and the extension group to present their special work to the class (extension group – monologues, support group – speech and thought bubbles). Ask the class to comment on the perception of the participants in thinking about how different characters would think and feel in certain situations. How would the extension group's monologue idea impact on the storyline of the play?	**Support:** give a small group one of the freeze-frame photographs and ask them to write speech and thought bubbles to indicate what each character is thinking/saying **Extend:** ask a small group to prepare a longer speech for one of the characters in their story to say in the middle of their play. This could be a monologue where the action freezes and the audience focuses on one character acting and speaking his/her thoughts

Guided reading and writing

Give the group part of a well-known story to read. Ask them to read it through by themselves first. Now lead a discussion about how they could turn this into a playscript.

Assessment

Give a group of children a playscript. Ask them, with no support from you, to organise themselves into a team of actors with one of them being director.

Firstly they should read the play on their own, then hold a discussion where they discuss characteristics and motives of each character. The director then casts the play (decides who plays which part).

They then read through the play. The director can stop the action and give guidance about interpretation.

Observe the group and be on hand if they need any help.

Refer back to the learning outcomes on page 83.

Further work

Take the class to see a play in a theatre or invite an actor to school to talk to the class about the stages of developing a performance in a theatre and what strategies they use to learn their part.

DAY 1 ■ Puppet plays

Key features	Stages	Additional opportunities
Creative thinking: apply imaginative thinking to achieve an objective	### Introduction Collect together as many soft toys and puppets as you need for one per child. The children themselves could probably provide their own. Create a simple puppet theatre (a piece of cloth tied between two chairs). Invite two children to pick one toy/puppet each. Ask the class to give the toys names. Now ask them to think about a setting for the puppet play. Finally, they should give you an idea for a dilemma being faced by one or both of the characters. Invite the 'puppeteers' to improvise the scene by making the puppets 'come alive' in speech and movement. ### Speaking and listening Organise the class into pairs and give them a toy or puppet each. Ask them either to use the same scenario provided in the introduction or to develop their own ideas. Give them time to develop their play. Walk around the pairs helping them develop their puppet's movements, their vocal projection and continuity. ### Independent work Look together at some of the puppet plays. Ask the children to be critical of inaudibility or confused plot lines. Allow children to spend time revising their ideas. ### Plenary Discuss what the children thought of this activity. What was easy? What was difficult?	**Support:** adult support might be needed for a small group to help them organise their ideas; try to allow them to work as far as possible with their own ideas rather than relying on other people's **Extend:** a few confident children could take the role of 'vocal coaches' and help you by working with other groups who are having difficulty with voice projection

DAY 2 ■ Refining our ideas

Key features	Stages	Additional opportunities
Creative thinking: look at and think about things differently and from other points of view	### Introduction Remind the children about their improvised puppet plays from Day 1. Tell them they are going to refine and improve upon their plays in readiness to present them to a class of younger children (Reception/Year 1). What will they need to do to make them interesting to their young audience? Watch some extracts from puppet/animation shows for young children on DVD or video (copyright permitting). Can the children identify some important aspects of the programmes which are particularly relevant to making the programme suitable, such as slow, clear speech, repetition of action, opportunities for children to join in vocally, clearly defined characters (shown vocally and in the puppets' movements)? ### Independent work Give the children time to work on their puppet plays to make them suitable for young children to watch and enjoy. They could create props and musical sound effects to enhance the atmosphere of their play. They could record their ideas onto the simple storyboard on photocopiable page 96.	**Support:** record their dialogue beforehand then play it while concentrating on moving their puppets **Extend:** further develop the puppet play idea by creating a series of simple digital photographs of the action, and then creating a slideshow presentation which could be playing while they are performing their dialogue
Evaluation: evaluate the quality of an outcome	### Plenary Hold a dress rehearsal of the puppet plays. Encourage children to be positive about their own performances, but ask them to be 'critical friends' to each other if there are aspects which need to be improved.	

DAY 3 ■ Performances

Key features	Stages	Additional opportunities
	### Introduction You will need to enlist the help of a younger class in this session. The children are going to take their puppet/toy plays to perform to another class. If possible, organise for each pair of your children to be matched with a pair of children from the other class so that they can get together after the performances and discuss their reactions to the play.	**Support:** some children might be happier just performing to two or three younger children rather than the whole class
	### Speaking and listening Ask each pair of performers to introduce their characters to the audience, and give a brief outline of the setting and dilemma before their performance. Film parts of each performance. Try to capture some audience reaction as well. When the children have completed their performances invite the audience to give their first reactions to the plays they have seen. What did they like? What did they not like?	**Extend:** some children could record others' performances by using video and digital cameras
Evaluation: evaluate the quality of an outcome	### Independent work Back in the classroom show the footage you recorded. Invite the children's comments on their own and others' performances plus the reactions of the audience. Invite them to write some of their dialogue in the form of a script for other people to perform.	
	### Plenary Gather the class together and invite some children to read their scripts.	

Guided reading and writing

Invite a group of children to choose a playscript and organise themselves into a play reading group.
When they have finished, ask them to discuss the play together then individually write a review of it.

Assessment

Ask children to write a set of instructions which aim to help other Year 4 children to produce and perform a play for younger children.
Invite some of your children to devise a simple questionnaire for the class who watched the puppet plays to glean their feelings and thoughts about the play content, interest level and standard of performance.
Refer back to the learning outcomes on page 83.

Further work

Give a group the task of developing a puppet play for an older audience.
They could devise an initial questionnaire to find out the interests and expectations of their audience before deciding on their characters, setting and dilemma.
Invite an audience into the classroom to watch the finished play and ask them for their reactions afterwards.

DAY 1 ■ 'Pick a card, any card!'

Key features	Stages	Additional opportunities
	Introduction Recap with the children on the features of playscripts. Tell them they are going to create their own playscripts over the next three days. Have prepared beforehand some character, setting, dilemma cards in three piles. Invite three children to come to the front to choose one card from each of the piles. Child 1 should have the two characters child 2 the setting and child 3 the dilemma. Can the three children improvise a very short dialogue between the two characters (one line each) with the third acting as director/narrator?	**Support:** record their dialogue using a tape recorder
Creative thinking: apply imaginative thinking to achieve an objective	**Speaking and listening** Organise the class into groups of three. Each group takes a characters, setting and dilemma card. They should spend some time developing their dialogue confining themselves to one line each, then improvising a scene to show the dialogue in action.	**Extend:** make up their own characters, setting and dilemma cards and try them out on each other; these could be laminated and used for future drama lessons as a warm-up
	Independent work Ask individual children to write the dialogue from their improvised 'one liner' scenes in the form of a playscript.	
	Plenary Take some of the dialogue one liner playscripts and invite children to read them to the class. Invite comments and ideas for improvement.	

DAY 2 ■ Improvisation versus playscripts!

Key features	Stages	Additional opportunities
	Introduction Read *Granny I'm home* from the CD-ROM with the class. Now invite volunteers to read the parts of Gran and Bunda. Discuss what the two 'actors' will need to do to show their age, characters, moods and so on. For example: Gran will have an older, lower, slower voice; Bunda's voice will be loud, shrill and excited.	**Support:** chant nursery rhymes in different ways, such as quietly but clearly, loudly but creepily, slowly, quickly
Creative thinking: look at and think about things differently and from other points of view	**Speaking and listening** Give half the class, in pairs, copies of *Granny I'm home* and invite them to read the play in character as Bunda and Gran. Encourage them to try and 'move' the scene using the stage directions and their own initiative. Ask the other half, in pairs, to improvise the same scene without the script – following the storyline now familiar to the children. After some time rehearsing, invite pairs to perform their work. Alternate script readers and improvisers. What do the children in each group feel about their performances? Write some good things/bad things about each approach on the board, for example *script gives clear directions about how to act the parts, but it is difficult to act freely when you're holding a script.*	**Extend:** ask some children to learn a speech from a play by heart; invite them to perform their speech to the rest of the class (perhaps in the school hall); invite comments based on agreed criteria, such as clarity, tone
	Independent work/Plenary Voice projection is hugely important when acting in a play. If you can't hear the words, the play is ruined. Talk about pronunciation, breathing and pace of delivery. Give the children time to read a paragraph of simple text then ask for volunteers to read it in their projected voices.	

DAY 3 ■ Planning playscripts

Key features	Stages	Additional opportunities
	Introduction The next three sessions will give the children time to focus on improvising, planning and writing a playscript of their own. Recap on the strategies and rules of script writing to ensure everyone is clear about why scripts are important when planning a play, what needs to be included in a playscript to make it work, how to write a playscript, what is the intended audience? Decide before this lesson what stimulus you are going to give the children to help them develop their ideas, perhaps well-known stories or a famous painting or photograph.	**Support:** give some pairs of children story props to help them plan their play **Extend:** invite a group to invent a murder mystery game for a party; they could devise characters cards, dilemmas, settings
Creative thinking: discover and make connections through play and experimentation	**Speaking and listening** Give pairs of children time to discuss the task and to decide on a basic storyline for their plays. What is the genre going to be? Encourage them to use drama strategies to help them 'step into the world' of their imagination and explore and experiment with their ideas and storylines.	
Information processing: record information using formats they have devised	**Independent work** Decide whether you want the children to write their playscripts in pairs or individually. Give them time to make notes for their plays using either their own skeleton plans or photocopies of the story mountains used in earlier units. At this stage they should only be planning the skeleton of their play not the details	
	Plenary Check that the children are using beginning, build-up, dilemma/climax, resolution model. Read some of the script storylines and discuss the ideas.	

DAY 4 ■ Playscripts – the characters

Key features	Stages	Additional opportunities
	Introduction Read some examples of opening scenes in plays. What are the features? For example: introducing the characters and the setting. Draw attention to the formalities of the script: character lists, stage directions, how to write each character's words	**Support:** give a group of children a set of photographs of different people; they then select one each and discuss with adult support what their chosen character might be doing, feeling, thinking, about to do, have just done
Creative thinking: generate imaginative ideas in response to stimuli	**Speaking and listening** In pairs, invite children to decide on the main characters for their story, their names, their relationship to each other. Then they will be ready to flesh the characters out by hot-seating each other in role as one of the characters.	
	Independent work Invite the children to draw their characters and annotate the pictures with notes and ideas to remind them about their characteristics, personalities and the role they are going to play in the story. They could use a simple grid with headings of: *Character's name, Appearance, Characteristics, Actions.*	
	Plenary Ask some children to introduce themselves to the class in role as one of their characters. Can they transform into the character, thinking like them, talking like them moving, like them? Encourage the class to ask the character questions. Are they asking searching and interesting questions?	

DAY 5 ▪ Playscripts - the action

Key features	Stages	Additional opportunities
Evaluation: express their own views, opinions and preferences	**Introduction** Revisit the play extract *Granny I'm home!* Look together at the stage directions. Can the children pick out the author's use of adverbs to guide the actors playing the parts by giving them clear ideas about the character's mood, feelings and vocal tone at any point in the play, for example *waves the book triumphantly; laughing happily.* Give the class time to look through copies of the play extract and underline other examples of adverbs in the stage directions. **Speaking and listening** Ask the children to refer back to their playscript planning and work on improvising the first scene of their play. Remind them not to 'ramble on' but to use the discipline of 'one liners' – each character saying one thing. **Independent work** Encourage the children to write the first scene in playscript format. Remind them to keep the character's speech down to a minimum. Walk around the room checking they are confident in their playscript layout and advising on good use of adverbs in the stage directions. **Plenary** Some children will complete this task. Using their scripts, invite other children to read the parts, following the author's directions as far as possible. Invite suggestions for improvement.	**Support:** some children will need to work with an adult to help them organise their ideas and develop their improvisations **Extend:** some children could work in pairs to learn the lines of the characters in a playscript and then perform the play to enable everyone to see the next stage after the initial reading and 'walk through'

DAY 6 ▪ Completing our playscripts

Key features	Stages	Additional opportunities
	Introduction Have prepared an example of someone's opening playscript scene on the board. Remind the children about the disciplines of playwriting. Ask them to read the playscript together and identify good examples of descriptive stage directions, characterisations and quality speech. **Speaking and listening** The pairs improvise the climax and resolutions to their play. Ask them to join with another pair and encourage the pairs to show their work to each other.	**Support:** some children will need help in writing their ideas
Information processing: record information using formats they have devised	**Independent work** Give the children time to write the climax and resolutions to their plays. Work with individuals offering suggestions, supporting their ideas and encouraging them to refine their ideas.	**Extend:** some children will complete their scripts quickly. Ask them to think about what props, sound effects and costumes they would need if they were going to stage the play
Evaluation: evaluate the quality of an outcome	**Plenary** Talk with the children about the possibility of putting on a performance of some of the class plays to another class or in an assembly. Discuss the implications of this – rehearsal schedules, casting parts, costumes, props and so on. Invite children to volunteer their scripts for consideration. Hold some play readings and ask the class to be the 'selection panel' to choose two or three plays for the class performances. Decide before the selection process what the criteria is for selection, for example number of cast, good stage directions, interesting storyline.	

Guided reading

Ask a group to read a playscript together. Bring the play alive for a performance of an extract at the end of the week. Choose a different playscript for each of the groups (according to ability).

A support staff member could help each group develop their characters and some actions.

Assessment

Read a play together with the children.

How familiar are they with the format of playscripts? Do they try to follow the stage directions? Do they know only to read the dialogue allocated to their character? Are they attempting to develop characterisation in their vocal and physical performance?

Give them the CD-ROM assessment activity 'Playscript' and ask them to write their own play. Provide less confident children with a word bank, if required.

Refer back to the learning outcomes on page 83.

Further work

Either take the class to the theatre to see a play or organise for a theatre company to come to school.

If possible ask one or more of the actors/ backstage people to talk to the children about the role they play in producing a play. The children could prepare questions beforehand in groups, with a spokesperson to ask the questions on the day.

Playscripts

◼ Use this page to help you plan your playscript.

Play Title:	
Characters' names	Character descriptions
1.	
2.	
Stage directions:	

Scene number:	
Character 1	Character's speech
Character 2	Character's speech
Character 1	Character's speech
Character 2	Character's speech

◼ 100 LITERACY FRAMEWORK LESSONS YEAR 4

PHOTOCOPIABLE ◼SCHOLASTIC
www.scholastic.co.uk

Stage directions

Jump in the air laughing with delight.	Curl up on the floor crying.
Run and hide in terror.	Double up with laughter.
Scream in shock.	Look shy.
Creep furtively.	Stare angrily.
Gasp with delight.	Look embarrassed.
Exit proudly.	Enter excitedly.

Storyboard

◼ Record your ideas for your play on this sheet.

Image 1	Image 2	Image 3	Image 4
Text			
Sound effects			
Props			
Stage directions			

NON-FICTION
UNIT 1 Recounts: newspapers/magazines

Speak and listen for a range of purposes on paper and on screen

Strand 1 Speaking
- Tell stories effectively and convey detailed information coherently for listeners.

Strand 2 Listening and responding
- Compare the different contributions of music, words and images in short extracts from TV programmes.

Read for a range of purposes on paper and on screen

Strand 7 Understanding and interpreting texts
- Deduce characters' reasons for behaviour from their actions and explain how ideas are developed in non-fiction texts.

Strand 8 Engaging with and responding to texts
- Interrogate texts to deepen and clarify understanding and response.

Write for a range of purposes on paper and on screen

Strand 9 Creating and shaping texts
- Develop and refine ideas in writing using planning and problem-solving strategies.
- Use settings and characterisation to engage reader's interest.

Strand 10 Text structure and organisation
- Organise texts into paragraphs to distinguish between different information, events or processes.

Strand 12 Presentation
- Use word-processing packages to present written work and continue to increase speed and accuracy in typing.

Progression in recounts

In this year children are moving towards:
- Analysing and identifying the features of recount texts based on real events from the Second World War; asking and answering: who, what, where, when?
- Demonstrating how to write a simple recount, identifying use of first person and past tense before applying these features in a draft form as a basis for later work.
- Reading and discussing the concepts of 'fact' and 'opinion' in both recounts and an example newspaper article.
- Analysing newspaper texts revising key organisational features and identifying language conventions; redrafting recounts into newspaper articles.
- Studying a visual text as the basis for a newspaper article; using drama to study and record character opinions alongside factual evidence; planning, drafting and writing a newspaper article that contains both factual and opinion-based content.

UNIT 1 ◄ Recounts: newspapers/magazines *continued*

Key aspects of learning covered in this Unit

Creative thinking
Children will be encouraged to use their historical knowledge and their imaginations to create a setting and a new story set in the past (Second World War).

Empathy
Exploring historical settings and events through narrative will help children to develop a sense of empathy with historical characters (evacuees in the Second World War) and an understanding of their way of life.

Self-awareness
Children will discuss and reflect on their personal responses to texts.

Communication
Children will often work collaboratively in pairs and groups. They will communicate outcomes orally, in writing and using other modes and media where appropriate.

Prior learning

Before starting this Unit check that the children can:
- Identify past tense verb form.
- Recall and record simple events in chronological order.
- Identify time related vocabulary.
- Recognise first and third person forms.

If they need further support please refer to a prior Unit or a similar Unit in Year 3.

Resources

Phase 1:
Information texts on evacuation, such as *At Home in World War 2 – Evacuation* by Stewart Ross; Photographs of evacuees ❦; *Letter to Grandma* by Sue Graves (including differentiated version) ❦; Recount skeleton ❦; Fiction and non-fiction texts about the Second World War, such as *The Diary of a Young Girl* by Anne Frank and *Carrie's War* by Nina Bawden; Photocopiable page 113 'Evacuation day'; Interactive activity 'Evacuation day' ❦

Phase 2:
My Christmas shoes and *Santa's gift to evacuees* by Sue Graves ❦; Information texts on the Second World War and evacuation; Photographs of evacuees on a train ❦; Photocopiable page 114 'Fact or opinion?'

Phase 3:
Welsh words of welcome! and *School's out!* by Sue Graves ❦; Suitable current newspaper stories and magazine articles; Photograph of evacuees having tea ❦; Diaries and personal recounts of the Second World War; Photocopiable page 115 'Newspaper article' and/or interactive activity 'Evacuees at village school' ❦

Phase 4:
Photographs of evacuees on a farm, and sheltering in a trench ❦; Copies of newspaper articles from the Second World War; Word-processing or desktop publishing software; Photocopiable page 116 'Key words and events'; Assessment photograph of evacuees being registered ❦

Cross-curricular opportunities

History – the Second World War

UNIT 1 ■ Teaching sequence

Phase	Children's objectives	Summary of activities	Learning outcomes
1	I can read and retrieve information. I can put events into the right order. I can draft a letter.	Create a timeline. Reorder visual information to tell a story. Create/edit timeline of a recount. Draft recount (letter).	Children can sequence events. Children can sequence a recount. Children can identify key events; write a draft in the correct verb tense.
2	I can discuss what I have read. I can evaluate and draw conclusions from what I have read or seen in a picture. I can tell the difference between a fact and an opinion.	Write facts/opinions. Write a reflective evaluation. Write a conclusion to the recount. Highlight key factual evidence. Make a commentary on the visual image.	Children can orally, and in writing, distinguish between facts and opinions. Children can comment on a recount draft. Children can identify and record factual information and opinions.
3	I can identify key language features. I can compare what I have read with other texts. I can make notes. I can organise my writing into paragraphs. I can discuss and write a newspaper article from a recount.	Identify newspaper features. Find similarities and differences between articles. Make notes and rough drafts. Write recounts from notes drafts. Turn recounts into newspaper articles. Write newspaper articles from recounts.	Children can identify the key language and presentational features of newspaper articles. Children can identify the key similarities and differences between recounts and newspaper articles. Children can draft a newspaper article based on a recount.
4	I can get information from a photograph. I can discuss different perceptions. I can plan and draft a newspaper article. I can use ICT to publish a text.	Record factual evidence. Use drama to explore perceptions. Record opinions. Write newspaper article. Publish work.	Children can record evidence. Children can understand different character perceptions. Children can plan, draft and use ICT to publish a newspaper article.

Provide copies of the objectives for the children.

DAY 1 ▪ Retrieving information

Key features	Stages	Additional opportunities
	Introduction Find out what the children know about the Second World War. Where did they get their information from? Examples might be old newspapers, magazines, books, films. Read, for example, chapter 1 of *At Home in World War 2 – Evacuation* by Stewart Ross explaining the events leading to war and the need to evacuate children from the most vulnerable areas. Take the opportunity to practise using the index to find out additional information for this topic, for example on *bombing, evacuation, blitz*.	**Phonics:** split unfamiliar words into phonemes for reading **HFWs:** house, home **MFWs:** began, started
Creative thinking: use imagination **Social skills:** turn-taking	**Speaking and listening** Ask the children to imagine that they were to be evacuated from their homes. How would they feel? Encourage them to take turns and not to interrupt while others are speaking. Examine the timeline of page 4 of the book. Point out that not all the information relates entirely to the sequence of the evacuations. Discuss how the text could be edited to give the key events of the evacuations only.	
	Independent work Invite the children to write their own timelines about the evacuations based on what they have read.	
	Plenary Bring the class back together. Choose children to show their work to the others. Can the others suggest alternatives or improvements?	

DAY 2 ▪ Telling a story

Key features	Stages	Additional opportunities
	Introduction Ask the children to recall the previous day's lesson. Choose a child to tell you why children were evacuated during the Second World War.	**Phonics:** using phonic skills for writing **HFWs:** after, that, next, then **MFWs:** first, follow, number
	Speaking and listening Display the photograph of children being evacuated, from the CD-ROM. Ask the children to discuss the photograph to explain what is happening. Encourage them to respond appropriately to your prompt questions of who, what, when, where, why? Point out that your prompts will help them to tell a story.	
Communication: work collaboratively to tell a story	**Independent work** Organise the children into pairs. Ask them to discuss the photograph and to decide on a story. Invite one child to act as scribe. Give them 15 minutes for this activity.	**Support:** help children with sequencing
	Plenary After 15 minutes, bring the class back together. Choose two or three pairs of children to read their work to the others. Ask the rest of the class for feedback and comments on the stories.	

DAY 3 ■ Sequencing events

Key features	Stages	Additional opportunities
	Introduction Ask the children how we find out things about the past. Point out that old letters and diaries are good ways of finding out about people's lives from long ago. Display the evacuee's *Letter to Grandma* from the CD-ROM.	**Phonics:** Use the knowledge of phonics to decode unfamiliar words **HFWs:** we, were, mum, said. **MFWs:** didn't, know, told
Empathy: explore the feelings of historical characters through narrative	**Speaking and listening** Read the letter together and discuss its contents. Do the children think Roy and Jack were happy or not? Ask them to give reasons for their answers. Point out the use of the past tense when Roy recounts the evacuation. Point out the chronological sequence to the evacuation. Invite the children to locate sequential steps to make a timeline. Demonstrate how to use the timeline to draw out key events using the Recount skeleton from the CD-ROM.	**Support:** use the differentiated text
	Independent work Invite the children to write their own timelines for Roy and Jack's evacuation based on the example you have modelled.	
	Plenary Bring the class back together. Ask some children to show their work to the others. Prompt them to justify the information they have included on their timelines. Together complete the text type skeleton on screen using examples from the children's work. You may want to keep a copy for reference.	

DAY 4 ■ Drafting a recount: letter

Key features	Stages	Additional opportunities
	Introduction Encourage the children to recall the previous lesson. Ask them what sort of text type they have been studying.	
Creative thinking: use imagination and historical knowledge	**Speaking and listening** Re-read *Letter to Grandma* from the CD-ROM. Can the children identify the key events in the evacuation? Ask them to identify the verb tense in the evacuation description. On the board, demonstrate how to write a recount based on the one read. Take the opportunity to point out the conventions of letter-writing. Include a 'Who? What? Where? When? Why' introduction. Invite the children to imagine that they are evacuees in the Second World War and that they are writing a letter to a parent, grandparent or friend telling them about their first day in their new foster home. What key information would they include?	**Support:** identify verb tenses
	Independent work Ask the children to draft their own letters. Remind them to use the correct verb tense. They may refer to information texts in books or on the Internet to help them.	**Extend:** locate information using a variety of sources
Communication: group discussion	**Plenary** Bring the class back together at the end of the session. Select three children to read aloud their work. Have they focused their writing on key events? Invite the others to suggest alternatives where appropriate.	

Guided reading

The children may want to read a range of books about the Second World War to find out how children's lives were affected by it. The following two books are suggested for both guided and independent reading: *The Diary of a Young Girl* by Anne Frank and *Carrie's War* by Nina Bawden.

Assessment

At the end of this Phase, ask the children to identify the features of a recount text. Check their work for evidence that they can sequence events chronologically in recounts and that they can draft their own recounts independently.

Refer back to the learning outcomes on page 99.

Further work

This Phase can be extended by inviting the children to examine diaries of people who lived during the Second World War, for example, Anne Frank. Encourage the children to draft their own diary entries of that time, based on texts they have read.

Use photocopiable page 113 'Evacuation day' or the interactive version from the CD-ROM to support children who need help sequencing recount texts. Remind them that recounts are written in chronological order.

DAY 1 ■ Facts and opinions

Key features	Stages	Additional opportunities
Empathy: explore historical events and settings to develop understanding	**Introduction** Ask the children to tell you what they have learned about the lives of evacuees during the Second World War. Display *My Christmas shoes parts 1* and *2* from the CD-ROM. Together read the extract. Take the opportunity to revisit features of a recount text, such as verb tenses and chronological order. **Speaking and listening** Spend time talking about the extracts you have just read. What were the good and bad parts of the day especially for the writer's little brother? Remind the children to take turns and to listen while others are speaking. Discuss what is meant by 'fact' and 'opinion'. Invite the children to find examples from the extract. **Independent work** Invite the children to write down three facts from the extract and three opinions. Tell them that you will give them ten minutes to complete this task. Remind them to write clearly and in sentences. **Plenary** Bring the class back together. Invite about four children to share their work with the rest of the class. Does everyone agree with their choices of facts and opinions? How many made different choices? Why?	**Phonics:** segment words into phonemes for spelling **Support:** identify verbs and tenses; use photocopiable page 114 'Fact or opinion?' to support the difference between fact and opinion **Extend:** express opinions

DAY 2 ■ Evaluating a recount

Key features	Stages	Additional opportunities
Self-awareness: discuss and reflect on response to a narrative	**Introduction** Recall the previous lesson. What is the difference between a fact and an opinion? Ask the children to give examples of each. **Speaking and listening** Display *My Christmas shoes parts 1* and *2* from the CD-ROM. Re-read the texts together. Ask the children to evaluate the recount. Provide prompts to help them discuss this appropriately, for example, do they think this is an entirely factual piece or an opinion? Do they feel that this extract tells them more about the lives of evacuees? Why/why not? Demonstrate on the board how to plan, draft and write a reflective evaluation of the extract. Encourage the children to make suggestions during this process. **Independent work** Ask the children to plan, draft and write their own evaluation of the extract modelling their work on the example done in class. (If wished, this task can be done over two or three days.) **Plenary** Invite two children to show their work to the others. Does the rest of the class feel that the evaluations are accurate? How could they be improved? Rewrite the evaluation you demonstrated on the board to include the best ideas from the children's work.	**Phonics:** split words into phonemes for spelling **HFWs:** it, is, not **MFWs:** think, know, knew

DAY 3 ■ Writing a new ending for a recount

Key features	Stages	Additional opportunities
	Introduction Ask the children how they evaluated the extract from the previous lesson. What processes did they have to go through, for example plan, draft and write?	**MFWs:** didn't, brother, mother
Empathy: read about characters and discuss	**Speaking and listening** Display *My Christmas shoes parts 1* and *2* from the CD-ROM. Refer the children to the last paragraph. Point out that the extract ends with the writer's opinion that it was a lovely day, and one that she will always remember. Do the children think that the little brother would have had the same opinion of the day? Why not? Spend time talking about a conclusion for the extract that would reflect the little brother's opinion as well as that of the writer. Which facts from the extract could they draw on to help them write their conclusion? Encourage the children to analyse the text carefully to find facts to support their opinions.	**Extend:** use facts to support opinions
Creative thinking: use historical knowledge and imagination to write a story	**Independent work** Invite the children to write their own conclusions to the extract which include the little brother's concepts of how the day went.	**Support:** use phonic skills for spelling
	Plenary Ask a child to read out his or her conclusion. Ask the others to listen carefully to check that the conclusion incorporates the little brother's opinion of the day as well as the writer's. How could the conclusion be improved? Encourage the rest of the class to make suggestions.	

DAY 4 ■ Finding facts in a newspaper article

Key features	Stages	Additional opportunities
	Introduction Remind the children of the extract they have been studying about the evacuee and her Christmas shoes. Explain that they are now going to read a newspaper article about the same event.	
Self-awareness: reflect and discuss	**Speaking and listening** Display the newspaper article *Santa's gift to evacuees* from the CD-ROM. Before reading point out the features of a newspaper article and in particular the way it is presented. Together read aloud the extract. Take the opportunity to split difficult words into phonemes for reading. After reading the extract, ask the children if they think this is a factual piece or one based on opinion. Invite them to locate facts from the article.	**Extend:** fact-finding
	Independent work Hand out a copy of the extract to each child and provide them with highlighter pens. Ask them to highlight five facts in the piece. Give them five or six minutes to complete this task.	
	Plenary When the time is up, bring the children back together. Select children to show their selected facts. How many chose the same/different facts? Encourage the children to discuss the choices made and to ask relevant questions about them.	**Extend:** children ask relevant questions

DAY 5 ■ Separating fact from opinion

Key features	Stages	Additional opportunities
	Introduction Ask the children to recall the newspaper article they read yesterday. Did they think it was a factual article or an opinion? Take the opportunity to revisit newspaper features, such as the headline and eyewitness quotes.	
Self-awareness: discuss and reflect	**Speaking and listening** Display the photograph of a group of evacuees on a train from the CD-ROM. Ask the children to describe the boys on the train. Do they think they are really as happy as they look? Why? Discuss whether a photograph such as this can give facts, opinions or both. Point out that the photographer may have wanted to express his or her opinion of evacuees by choosing to take a picture of children smiling and waving. Discuss that our opinions might be affected by an author's or a photographer's commentary.	**Extend:** express opinions
	Independent work Organise the children into groups. Provide each group with one or two books containing images of evacuees during the Second World War. Ask them to select pictures that give factual information. Tell them they have ten minutes to complete this task.	**Support:** help children locate information in non-fiction texts
	Plenary Ask members from each group to show their choices to the rest of the class. What facts have they found out from the pictures? Have the pictures affected their opinions of evacuees and evacuation? Encourage further discussion and questioning.	**Extend:** ask relevant questions

Guided reading

Invite the children to research facts about children in the Second World War on the internet and in books. What have they found out about their lives at that time? How do children's lives today differ from the lives of children then?

Ask the children to find examples of fact and opinion about the lives of children at that time. Invite them to share their findings.

Assessment

Ask the children to tell you the differences between a fact and an opinion. Is a 'fact' the truth or not? If someone gives an opinion, is it always the truth? Why/why not? Encourage the children to give you examples of fact and opinion from their reading. Keep a record of the children's abilities to identify the differences.

Refer back to the learning outcomes on page 99.

Further work

This Phase can be extended by examining books about the Second World War such as *Witness to History – World War 2* by Sean Connelly (Heinemann Library). This book contains personal recounts of events during the war. However, as the author points out, personal accounts tell the truth 'but only so far as the writer can know it.'

Ask the children to examine personal accounts to identify examples of fact and opinion. Ask them to share their findings with the rest of the class.

DAY 1 ▣ Features of newspaper articles

Key features	Stages	Additional opportunities
	Introduction Explain to the children that they are going to be examining more newspaper articles in this next Phase. Take the opportunity to find out how many read newspapers. What can they tell you about the way they are presented? What tense are they usually written in?	**Extend:** take class surveys of newspapers read
Communication: work collaboratively	**Speaking and listening** Display *Welsh words of welcome!* from the CD-ROM. Together read the article. After reading ask the children to tell you what the article is about. Invite them to find examples of newspaper features, for example headline, quotes, paragraphs, columns and so on.	
Reading: locate features	**Independent work** Hand out copies of current newspaper articles together with blank A4 paper. Ask the children to locate the following features in the newspapers: headline, column, paragraph, quote; an example of the past tense and use of the third person. Ask them to cut out their examples and paste them onto the A4 sheets. They should label their examples accordingly.	**Support:** help children with labelling
	Plenary Invite children to show their work to the rest of the class. Encourage the others to check for accuracy and to suggest alternatives where appropriate.	

DAY 2 ▣ Comparing newspaper articles

Key features	Stages	Additional opportunities
	Introduction Encourage the children to recall the work you did yesterday on newspapers. Choose children to identify the critical features of a newspaper article.	**Phonics:** spelling patterns for the long vowel phoneme *a-e*: same; identifying syllabic patterns in multi-syllabic words
Communication: work collaboratively	**Speaking and listening** Display *Welsh words of welcome!* from the CD-ROM. Spend time checking that the children understand the critical features discussed in the introduction and can identify them. Now display *School's out!* from the CD-ROM showing another imaginary newspaper article from the Second World War. Read the article together. Ask the children to help you examine the two articles using a graphic organiser. Ask them to compare the headings. Point out that one is alliterative whereas the other has a double meaning. *School's out!* could mean the children are having a holiday. However, in this case the message is that the children are having their lessons outside.	**Support:** locate critical features of a newspaper article
	Independent work Ask the children to make lists of features that are the same/different between the two articles. Give them ten minutes to complete the task.	
	Plenary When the time is up, call the children together. Ask two or three children to share their work with the others. Encourage discussion about their choices of similarities and differences.	**Extend:** justify their choices

DAY 3 ■ Making notes for a recount

Key features	Stages	Additional opportunities
	Introduction Invite the children to discuss the critical features of a newspaper article and a recount. What are the differences between them? Point out the use of the first person and past tense in a recount and the use of the third person and past tense in a newspaper article.	**Support:** analyse different types of texts for verbs and past tenses; split words into phonemes for spelling
Empathy: explore photographs **Creative thinking:** use historical knowledge and imagination	**Speaking and listening** Display the photograph from the CD-ROM that shows a group of evacuees sitting down for supper for the first time with their new foster mother. Discuss the picture. How do the children think the evacuees feel? Are they frightened, excited, homesick? Now ask the children to choose a child from the photograph and to name him. Ask them to help you write a recount as if written by their chosen child. Take the opportunity to remind them about the use of the first person and the past tense.	
	Independent work Invite the children to choose the other child from the picture and to make notes and, if time, a rough draft of a recount by him. Tell them you will give them 15 minutes for this task.	
	Plenary Ask three children to discuss their notes/ drafts. Invite the rest of the class to check for accuracy and offer suggestions.	

DAY 4 ■ Drafting and writing a recount

Key features	Stages	Additional opportunities
	Introduction Remind the children of the work they did yesterday on analysing features of recounts. Select one or two children to read out the notes they made yesterday to check that they have created a chronological sequence to their recounts.	**HFWs:** and, but, because, so **Support:** check for chronological sequencing in recounts; encourage children to split difficult words into phonemes for spelling
Grammar: conjunctions, adverbs	**Speaking and listening** Take the opportunity to revise conjunctions and adverbs and their importance in establishing cohesion within paragraphs. Ask them to compose sentences that contain conjunctions and adjectives. Spend time talking about the importance of organising their recounts into paragraphs. Using their notes to help them ask the children what they would include in one of their paragraphs.	
	Independent work Now ask the children to write their recounts, bearing in mind the points raised earlier in the lesson. Give them about 20 minutes to complete this task.	
Communication: discuss outcomes	**Plenary** When the time is up, bring the children together. Invite four children to read aloud their recounts. Invite the others to check for accuracy and to offer suggestions for improving their work.	

DAY 5 ▪ A recount into a newspaper article (1)

Key features	Stages	Additional opportunities
	Introduction Explain to the children that they are going to help you turn a personal recount into a newspaper article. Display *Welsh words of welcome!* and *School's out!* from the CD-ROM to revise features of a newspaper article. Point out in particular the use of the third person.	
	Speaking and listening Now ask a volunteer to read aloud his or her recount from yesterday. Model how to change the recount into a newspaper article. Encourage the children to make suggestions. When the article is complete, choose a child to read it aloud. Do the others agree that it has all the critical features of a newspaper article? Encourage the children to locate paragraphs, past tense and use of the third person.	**Extend:** locate paragraphs, third person, past tense
Communication: work collaboratively in pairs; make suggestions to improve writing skills	**Independent work** Organise the children into pairs. Ask one child to write a personal recount of five sentences about attending a village school as an evacuee. Ask the second child to rewrite the sentences as a newspaper article. Allow the children 20 minutes for this task with each child spending ten minutes writing.	
	Plenary Choose three pairs of children to read their recounts and accompanying articles. Ask the others to check that each text type is accurately written.	

DAY 6 ▪ A recount into a newspaper article (2)

Key features	Stages	Additional opportunities
	Introduction Talk about the work done yesterday on recounts and newspaper articles. Ensure the children can recall the critical features of both text types.	**MFWs:** children, place, different, friend, mother, father
Communication: take part in class discussion	**Speaking and listening** Explain to the children that they are going to turn the recounts they wrote on Day 4 into newspaper articles, remembering to change the first person to the third person and to use the past tense. Spend time discussing the process needed for this task. Encourage all the children to participate in the discussion. If need be, practise changing one or two sentences from their recounts into the third person.	**Support:** revise past tense and use of first and third person
Self-awareness: discuss and reflect	**Independent work** Set the children to work on their task. Remind them to proofread their work and to check difficult spellings in their dictionaries or word bank books, if necessary. Tell the children you will allow them 20 minutes to complete this task.	**Support:** using dictionaries and word banks for spelling
	Plenary Ask three volunteers to read both their original recounts and their newspaper articles to the class. Have the children fulfilled the criteria for both text types? Invite the others to suggest alternatives where errors occur. Select a sample of completed work for a classroom display for demonstration of these text types.	

Guided reading

Invite the children to read a wide range of newspaper and magazine articles to reinforce the skills they have obtained during this Phase. Talk about what they have read. What key/critical features have they found in their reading?

Encourage them to make critical analyses of what they read including any key features.

Assessment

During a whole class teaching session, spend time checking that the children can recall the key features of a personal recount and a newspaper article. Encourage all the children to participate. Where difficulties arise revisit sections of the Phase to secure these skills.

Refer back to the learning outcomes on page 99.

Further work

Provide the children with copies of diaries and personal recounts of the Second World War. Invite the children to choose interesting entries from these recounts and turn them into newspaper articles. Use photocopiable page 115 'Newspaper article' or the interactive version from the CD-ROM 'Evacuees at village school' to provide extra support for turning a recount into a newspaper article.

DAY 1 ◼ Recording evidence

Key features	Stages	Additional opportunities
	Introduction Introduce this next Phase by checking that the children can recall the presentational features of a newspaper/magazine text. Encourage more reluctant participators in the class to contribute.	**HFWs:** first, then, next, after **MFWs:** first, jumped, eyes, around, above
Empathy: explore photographs	**Speaking and listening** Display the two pictures from the CD-ROM: the first shows evacuees working on a farm. The second shows a group of evacuees taking shelter in a trench on a farm while an air battle (dog fight) takes place above their heads. Discuss the photographs with the children. Ask them to relate a possible narrative sequence using the photographs as evidence. Use a graphic organiser to establish factual recount information based on the evidence in the photographs. Encourage all of the children to participate fully in this activity.	
	Independent work Invite the children to write independent factual recounts imagining that they are one of the children in the pictures. Remind them to record their recounts in the first person and in the past tense and to check their work on completion for good sentence structure and punctuation.	
	Plenary Choose two or three children to show their work to the others. Ask the rest of the class to check for accuracy, especially correct use of tense and first person.	

DAY 2 ◼ Putting yourself in someone else's shoes

Key features	Stages	Additional opportunities
	Introduction Ask the children to recall the previous day's lesson. What were the images that they wrote about?	
Self-awareness: explore different character perceptions	**Speaking and listening** Display the two pictures from the CD-ROM. Ask the children to imagine that they were one of the evacuees and that they were working on the farm when they were told to take cover. How did they feel? Were they frightened, excited, worried? Did they feel safe in the trench or vulnerable? Encourage the children to express their opinions and feelings clearly. Remind them also to take turns and not to interrupt while others are speaking.	**Support:** remind children to take turns and listen while others are speaking
Communication: work collaboratively	**Independent work** Organise the children into groups. Ask each group to act out the narrative shown in the images. Ask them to explore different character perceptions. Were some of the children bolder than others? Did any think it was very exciting? Allow the children 15 minutes to work on their dramatisations.	**Extend:** hot-seat the evacuees
	Plenary When the time is up, invite the groups to show their short dramatisations to the others. When all the groups have had a turn, spend time assessing the performances and talking about the different character perceptions that have been highlighted.	

DAY 3 — Recording opinions

Key features	Stages	Additional opportunities
Communication: discuss performances	**Introduction** Spend time talking about the children's performances from the previous day. Did they find it easy or difficult to put themselves into the evacuees' shoes?	**HFWs:** I, me, they, he , she **MFWs:** think, thought, knew, know
Self-awareness: analyse different character viewpoints	**Speaking and listening** Extend the above discussion by talking about the different character viewpoints that emerged from the drama activity. How did the viewpoints differ? What similarities were there? Ask the children to help you make notes on the board about the different character viewpoints.	**Support:** note writing skills, using key words and episodes; use phonic skills for writing
	Independent work Using the notes on the board, ask the children to record their opinions on the events they dramatised. Remind the children that this will form the basis of the next day's work when they will be writing a newspaper article. Tell the children that you will allow 20 minutes for the completion of this task.	
	Plenary Ask for a few volunteers to share their work with the rest of the class. Spend time discussing the work shared. How many others held similar opinions about the dramatised events? How many had opposing opinions? Encourage the children to question each other about why they reached a certain opinion.	**Extend:** ask relevant questions

DAY 4 — Writing a recount: newspaper article

Key features	Stages	Additional opportunities
	Introduction Revisit the work the children did yesterday. Talk about the way you prepared notes on the dramatisations together. Take the opportunity to revisit note-taking skills: using key words, picking out key events/episodes.	**Support:** use photocopiable page 116 'Key words and events' to practise note-taking skills
	Speaking and listening Tell the children that they will be using their notes as references for writing up their own newspaper articles based on the photographs from the CD-ROM. Re-open this screen to remind the children of the images. Discuss the images in depth. Discuss with the children what presentational features they will need to use to write a newspaper article. What verb tense will they use?	
Creative thinking: write a newspaper article based on notes	**Independent work** Ask the children to write their newspaper articles, using their notes and referring to the visual images on screen. Remind them to use appropriate language, to write in the third person and to use the past tense. Suggest that they may include quotes to support their articles.	**Support:** check verb tenses
	Plenary Invite some of the children to share their work with the others at the end of the session. Ask the others to check that appropriate language and presentational features have been used. Select examples of the children's work to display in the classroom.	**Extend:** use appropriate language in articles; presentational features

DAY 5 ■ Publishing a recount

Key features	Stages	Additional opportunities
	Introduction Ask the children about the work from the previous day. Spend time talking about the samples that have been displayed in the classroom. Talk about presentational features and the language used.	
	Speaking and listening Explain that the children will be publishing their articles as ICT texts during this lesson. Spend time talking about the task and how they will go about it. In particular ask them how they will select pictures to accompany the text. Encourage all the children to participate in this discussion. However, remind them not to call out but to wait for their turn to speak.	**Support:** ensure children take turns
Communication: work collaboratively	**Independent work** Split the class into pairs and invite them to choose one of their newspaper articles to publish as an ICT text. Tell the children to spend time first researching appropriate pictures to accompany their text (copyright permitting). Then ask them to publish their article.	**Extend:** develop research skills and practise caption writing
	Plenary At the end of the session bring the class back together. Select about four pairs of children to show their published ICT texts. Ask the children to point out use of topic- and genre-specific language, presentational features, use of the third person and use of the past tense. How many thought to include a caption for their picture? Choose samples of the children's work to add to the classroom display.	

Guided reading

Encourage the children to read copies of old newspaper articles from the time of the Second World War. If possible arrange for the children to visit a local library and access the archives to read local newspapers from that time.
Talk about what they have read. What fact have they discovered? How did the war affect their local areas? Take time to discuss their findings.

Assessment

Display the CD-ROM assessment photograph and ask the children to write a newspaper article based on it. They should include fact and opinion in their answers.
Refer back to the learning outcomes on page 99.

Further work

Invite the children to write a complete class newspaper as if it were from the days of the Second World War.
Split the class into 'departments' to write about different news stories. Encourage them to research their news first and to take notes before writing up the articles and publishing them as an ICT text.
Print out the finished paper and display it in school for other classes to read and enjoy.

Evacuation day

■ Mary was evacuated during the war. This is a recount of what happened, but the sentences are in the wrong order.

■ Read the sentences, cut them out and put them in the right order.

>✂ -

Mary and her dad waited for the train to come.

A lady met them. She looked at the label on Mary's coat.

Dad lifted Mary into a railway carriage.

Mary waved and waved to Dad from the carriage window until she couldn't see him any longer.

Mary and her dad got to the railway station at 8 o'clock in the morning.

At last the train arrived.

The train pulled out of the station.

She made a note of Mary's name on a big clipboard. She told them to wait for the train to arrive.

NON-FICTION ■ UNIT 1

Fact or opinion?

■ Write the following statements under the correct heading.

1. Many evacuees were evacuated to villages in the countryside a long way from their homes.

2. Evacuees were taken to places in the country where bombs were unlikely to fall.

3. Mrs Evans thought that all the evacuees were dirty.

4. A billeting officer helped to house evacuees with foster parents.

5. One farmer in the village said that he thought evacuees had stolen apples from his orchard.

6. Many evacuees wrote to their parents to tell them how they getting on.

7. Angie thought her mum had sent her away because she didn't want her anymore.

8. A journalist in July 1944 wrote that he thought London was no place for children because it was so dangerous.

Fact:

_____

_____

_____

_____

Opinion:

_____

_____

_____

_____

■ 100 LITERACY FRAMEWORK LESSONS YEAR 4

PHOTOCOPIABLE ■SCHOLASTIC

www.scholastic.co.uk

Name _____   Date _____

Newspaper article

■ Write the missing words to change this recount into a newspaper article.

My first day

My name is Mary Lang. I am an evacuee from London. I am eight-years-old. On Monday I went to the village school for the first time. This is what happened.

Miss Miller, the teacher took the register and told the class that there were too many children in school now and that some of us would have to attend school in the morning and some in the afternoon. I was told that I had to attend school in the mornings.

After that we did some sums and then Miss Miller read us a story about a horse called Black Beauty. At midday we had to go home so that the other children could take our places and have their lessons.

Evacuees At Village School

Eight year old _____ _____ from _____

went to the village school for the first time on _____.

Her new teacher _____ _____ took the

_____. Then she told the _____ that there were

too _____ _____ in school now. She said that

_____ of them would have to attend _____

in the mornings and that _____ would _____

_____ school in the _____. Mary Lang was told

she had to _____ school in the _____.

After that the children did _____. Then _____

_____ read them a story about a _____ called

_____ _____.

At _____ the children went _____ so that other

children could take _____ _____ and have their

_____.

Key words and events

■ Read the newspaper article below.

■ Highlight key words and key events and write them in the boxes below.

Children watch dramatic dog fight!

Children working on a farm in Little Denham last week were witnesses to a dramatic dog fight that took place in the skies above their farm.

The children had been working in different parts of the farm during the morning. Some were feeding the pigs, whilst others were helping with the harvest.

Brian Peters, an evacuee, from London said. "We were working hard, when suddenly we heard lots of planes overhead. Mr Finlay, the farmer, yelled to us to run to the trench. We ran to the trench as fast as we could. The planes were shooting at each other. The planes' engines were screaming as they dipped and dived in the skies. It was very exciting. I wasn't a bit scared."

When Mr Finlay and the children got to the trench, several other evacuees had already arrived. Mr Finlay said that many of the younger children were terrified. He said, "Some of the kids were crying and shaking with fear. I'm sure they thought they were going to die. I felt so sorry for them."

Write key words here.

Write key events here.

NON-FICTION
UNIT 2 Information texts

Speak and listen for a range of purposes on paper and on screen

Strand 1 Speaking
■ Tell stories effectively and convey detailed information coherently for listeners.

Strand 2 Listening and responding
■ Listen to a speaker, make notes on the talk and use notes to develop a role-play.

Strand 3 Group discussion and interaction
■ Take different roles in groups and use the language appropriate to them, including roles of leader, reporter, scribe and mentor.

Strand 4 Drama
■ Create roles showing how behaviour can be interpreted from different view points.

Read for a range of purposes on paper and on screen

Strand 7 Understanding and interpreting texts
■ Deduce characters' reasons for behaviour from their actions and explain how ideas are developed in non-fiction texts.

Strand 8 Engaging and responding to texts
■ Read extensively favourite authors/genres and experiment with other types of text.
■ Interrogate texts to deepen and clarify understanding and response.

Write for a range of purposes on paper and on screen

Strand 9 Creating and shaping texts
■ Develop and refine ideas in writing using planning and problem-solving strategies.
■ Summarise and shape material and ideas from different sources to write convincing and informative non-narrative texts.
■ Choose and combine words, images and other features for particular effects.

Strand 10 Text structure and organisation
■ Organise texts into paragraphs to distinguish between different information, events or processes.
■ Use adverbs and conjunctions to establish cohesion within paragraphs.

Strand 11 Sentence structure and punctuation
■ Clarify meaning and point of view by using varied sentence structure (phrases, clauses and adverbials).
■ Use commas to mark clauses and the apostrophe for possession.

Progression in information texts

In this year children are moving towards:
■ Preparing for factual research by reviewing what is known, what is needed, what is available and where one might search.
■ Routinely using dictionaries and thesauruses and sequencing words in alphabetical order.
■ Scanning texts to locate key words, phrases, headings, lists, bullet points, captions and key sentences – appraising their usefulness in supporting the reader to gain information effectively.

▶

UNIT 2 ◄ Information texts *continued*

- Identifying how paragraphs are used to organise information.
- Making notes and filling them out into connected prose.
- Presenting information from a variety of sources in one simple format.
- Developing and refining ideas in writing using planning and problem-solving strategies.
- Editing and explaining reasons for the editorial choices.

Key aspects of learning covered in this Unit

Creative thinking
Children will generate and extend imaginative ideas to explain a process. They will suggest hypotheses, responding imaginatively through drama and talk, and respond to problems to create a written outcome.

Self-awareness
Children will discuss and reflect on their personal responses to the texts.

Evaluation
Children will present information orally, diagrammatically and in writing. They will discuss success criteria, give feedback to others and judge the effectiveness of their own work.

Communication
Children will often work collaboratively in pairs and groups. They will communicate outcomes orally, in writing and using other modes and media where appropriate.

Prior learning

Before starting this Unit check that the children can:
- Identify the key features of simple recount and report texts.
- Express clear opinions about characters' responses to a range of settings.
If they need further support please refer to a prior Unit or a similar Unit in Year 3.

Resources

Phase 1:
Non-fiction books on the Second World War; Dictionaries and thesauruses; Alphabetically ordered texts including online and printed encyclopedias; *Clothing* ❧; Photocopiable page 130 'Dictionary work'; Photocopiable page 131 'Famous people in the Second World War'; Interactive activity 'Dictionary, thesaurus, index or glossary?' ❧

Phase 2:
Digging for victory ❧; Texts on rationing and food in the Second World War; Photocopiable page 132 'Food in the Second World War'

Phase 3:
Photograph of children in gas masks ❧; Interactive activity 'Gas mask' ❧; Non-fiction texts on gas masks and air raid shelters; Assessment activity 'Shelters' ❧

Cross-curricular opportunities

History – the Second World War

UNIT 2 ■ Teaching sequence

Phase	Children's objectives	Summary of activities	Learning outcomes
1	I can use a dictionary. I can put words into alphabetical order. I know what synonyms are and can use a thesaurus to find them. I can find information in non-fiction texts. I can talk about the meanings of words.	Dictionary work. Thesaurus work. Write glossary definitions. Use appropriate information resources.	Children can prepare appropriately for factual research. Children can understand the purposes of glossary/index pages as an aid to research. Children can use glossaries/dictionaries to aid understanding of non-fiction texts.
2	I can scan a text to find useful information. I know that paragraphs are used to organise information. I can mark a text to highlight key information. I can research information and make notes. I can turn notes into connected prose. I can comment constructively on other people's work.	Scan and appraise a text. Mark and annotate a text. Write notes. Write connected prose from notes. Write notes collaboratively. Write connected prose collaboratively.	Children can assess the usefulness of a text in collecting information. Children can identify how paragraphs organise and sequence information. Children can make notes as an aid to writing. Children can use notes as an aid to writing. Children can work cooperatively to produce a piece of work.
3	I can discuss and examine information from a photograph. I can listen carefully to a reading and then make notes on what I have heard. I can take part in a role-play. I can discuss and listen to others opinions. I can discuss my work and edit it appropriately.	Create and label drawings. Make notes from reading. Role play, make notes. Write connected prose. Edit written work.	Children can examine a photograph then re-present the information in a simple format Children can present information in note form. Children can present information in a simple way through role play. Children can write connected prose. Children can develop and refine ideas in writing.

Provide copies of the objectives for the children.

DAY 1 ◢ Dictionary work

Key features	Stages	Additional opportunities
	### Introduction Introduce this Unit by explaining that we can research information from many different sources. Point out that sometimes words in non-fiction texts are unfamiliar to us and that we can use dictionaries to help us understand their meanings. Establish that dictionaries are organised alphabetically. Demonstrate on the board how to use second, third and fourth place letters to locate and sequence words in a dictionary.	**Support:** ensure children know the alphabet
	### Speaking and listening Ensure that each child has access to a dictionary. Invite the children to think of difficult words that they have met in Unit 1 on the Second World War, for example: *evacuation, evacuee, bombing*. Ask them to search for these words in their dictionaries. Choose different children to read out each definition as they find them.	
	### Independent work Provide the children with copies of photocopiable page 130 'Dictionary work'. Ask them to place the words in 'dictionary order' and to match them with their correct definitions. Allow 15 minutes for this task.	**Extend:** write their own definitions
Communication: work collaboratively	### Plenary At the end of the session ask the children to swap their work with their neighbour. Ask everyone to check their neighbour's work. Are the words ordered correctly and placed with the right definitions?	

DAY 2 ◢ Thesaurus work

Key features	Stages	Additional opportunities
	### Introduction Ask the children what they recall about the previous day's lesson. Check they remember how dictionaries are ordered. Spend time practising locating words using second, third and fourth letters.	**Phonics:** split words into phonemes for reading and spelling
	### Speaking and listening Ask the children about the uses of a thesaurus. Explain that it, too, is ordered alphabetically. Point out that often by finding a synonym it is easier to understand the meaning of unfamiliar words. Ask the children to suggest words that they have met so far in Units 1 and 2 about the Second World War that they think are difficult – examples might be *ration, billet* and so on. Encourage all the children to participate. They may refer to non-fiction books for unfamiliar words. Write their suggestions on the board.	
	### Independent work Now challenge the children to order the words on the board alphabetically. Having done this, ask them to find synonyms for the words. Allow them 15 minutes for this task. Remind them to proofread their work to check for spelling accuracy.	**Support:** help children with locating words in a thesaurus
Evaluation: present information and discuss	### Plenary Select children to show their work to the class. Ask the others to check for accuracy and to suggest alternatives where appropriate.	

DAY 3 ◼ Finding information in non-fiction texts

Key features	Stages	Additional opportunities
	Introduction Talk about finding information in non-fiction texts. Point out that the contents page, glossary and index all help us to research information books. Check that the children can locate each of these sections in non-fiction books.	**Phonics:** split words into phonemes for spelling
Evaluation: discuss, analyse differences **Communication:** make suggestions as a class	**Speaking and listening** Spend time talking about the different sections of a non-fiction book as mentioned above. Encourage the children to tell you the differences between each section. For example, what would they expect the index/glossary pages to tell them? Ask the children to list some Second World War terms. Demonstrate how to write a definition for one of the terms for a glossary. Encourage the children to help you with this.	
	Independent work Now ask the children to complete the glossary activity either on paper or the board. Remind them to check their spellings using a dictionary or spell-checker. Allow them ten minutes to complete this task.	**Support:** children use spell check or dictionaries to check spellings
	Plenary When the time is up, invite two or three children to read out their glossary terms to the others. Did the others write similar definitions? How did they differ? You could use the children's examples to complete the interactive activity from the CD-ROM.	

DAY 4 ◼ Finding the meanings of words

Key features	Stages	Additional opportunities
	Introduction Recap on the previous day's work. Discuss the different ways the children have located information in non-fiction texts. Remind them that glossaries, indexes, dictionaries and thesauruses are all ordered alphabetically.	**Phonics:** splitting multi-syllabic word into phonemes for reading and spelling
Self-awareness: read and discuss	**Speaking and listening** Display the extract *Clothing* from the CD-ROM and read it together. Discuss the text. What does it tell us about the shortages of goods during the war? What sort of clothes did the children then have to wear? Ask the class which words and phrases suggest that clothes were not readily available. Highlight the following words from the text: *little, clothing coupons, reuse, unravelled, re-knit*. Discuss the meaning of one of these words or phrases.	**Extend:** develop vocabulary
Communication: work collaboratively	**Independent work** Ask the children to work in pairs to find meanings of the other highlighted words. Invite one child of the pair to act as scribe while the other looks for meanings and definitions in a dictionary or glossary pages of books on the Second World War.	
	Plenary Ask two pairs of children to share their work. Does everyone agree with their definitions?	

Guided reading and writing

Encourage the children to read widely and to refer to dictionaries and glossaries to find the meanings of unfamiliar words. Spend time finding information about the Second World War quickly, practising using the index pages in non-fiction books. Invite the children to use the index page to find references. For example, on which pages can we find out about rationing? Extend this work by encouraging the children to make notes on the information they find on the listed pages.

Assessment

As a class, or in groups, complete the interactive activity: 'Dictionary, thesaurus, index or glossary?' Invite the children to drag and drop the items at the top of the page to place them under the correct heading. At the end of the assessment, check the children's level of understanding. Refer back to the learning outcomes on page 119.

Further work

Take the opportunity to examine other alphabetically ordered information texts, such as encyclopedias – both on screen and in book form. Encourage the children to find out additional information about famous people from the Second World War. Provide children with photocopiable page 131 'Famous people from the Second World War' for the children to record their findings about four famous people from this time. Tell the children they will be giving a talk about a person of their choice to the class, using notes they have made as aide-memoires.

DAY 1 ■ Collecting information

Key features	Stages	Additional opportunities
	Introduction Introduce this Phase by talking about the importance of getting food to people during the Second World War. Point out that people were encouraged to dig up their gardens and any pieces of spare ground in order to grow food. Explain that even children were encouraged to help grow food.	**Phonics:** use phonic skills to split words into phonemes for reading **HFWs:** read on sight: had, is to, was they, you, see
Self-awareness: read, discuss and respond to a text	**Speaking and listening** Display *Digging for Victory* from the CD-ROM. Read the extract together. Discuss the contents of the text. Encourage all the class to participate. Invite the children to scan the text to locate key words and sentences and identify other features. Invite the children to appraise their usefulness in helping the reader collect information.	
Communication: work collaboratively	**Independent work** Provide children with other texts on food rationing in the Second World War. Ask them to scan the texts to find the features you focused on in Speaking and listening above and to appraise the different texts. Allow the children to work in pairs.	**Support:** use a writing frame
	Plenary At the end of the session bring the children back together. Choose two pairs to share their work with the others. Ask the rest of the class to check the information supplied and to make comments on the appraisals.	

DAY 2 ■ Organising and sequencing information

Key features	Stages	Additional opportunities
Evaluation: appraise a text	**Introduction** Ask the children to recall the previous day's lesson. Can they remember what the extract was about? What features of the extract did they locate to help them appraise it. How did they appraise the usefulness of the features?	**Phonics:** split difficult words into phonemes for reading **HFWs:** read on sight: had, is to, was they, you, see
Self-awareness: read, discuss and respond to a text	**Speaking and listening** Display *Digging for Victory* from the CD-ROM and re-read the extract. Ask the children to tell you what a paragraph is. Select a child to identify a paragraph. Discuss how paragraphs are used to organise and sequence information. Mark and annotate paragraphs, inviting the children to help you. Take the opportunity to revisit conjunctions and adverbs, identifying them in the extract. Similarly point out phrases that clarify meaning, such as *Because of the loss of vital food supplies*. Invite the children to find other examples.	
	Independent work Provide children with copies of photocopiable page 132 'Food in the Second World War'. Ask them to mark and annotate key words, and sentences, headings and paragraphs. Tell them you will allow 10 minutes to complete this task.	
Communication: work collaboratively	**Plenary** At the end of the time, select four children to show their work to the class. Do the others agree with the marking and annotations made? What additional suggestions can they make?	

DAY 3 ■ Making notes

Key features	Stages	Additional opportunities
	Introduction Remind the children of the work they did yesterday. Ask them about the role of paragraphs in helping to organise and sequence information.	**Phonics:** using phonic skills for writing **Support:** grammar terms: paragraphs
Creative thinking: explain a process	**Speaking and listening** Display *Digging for victory* from the CD-ROM. Re-read the extract. Discuss how the author might have prepared when writing this chapter, for example doing research; making notes on the information he found before writing up his notes into connected prose. Discuss how to make notes. Encourage all the children to express their opinions about this. Encourage them to look for key words or to abbreviate ideas. Annotate the first paragraph to model how to make notes.	**Extend:** give opinions
	Independent work Leave *Digging for victory* on display for the children to refer to. Ask them to make notes on the remainder of the extract using your demonstration as a model. Remind them to bear in mind the order of the information as presented in the extract. Tell them they have 10 minutes to complete this activity.	**Support:** children make notes
Communication: share, discuss and appraise	**Plenary** When the time is up, bring the class back together. Ask three or four children to share their notes with the others. Ask them to analyse their work. Have they identified key words? Have they abbreviated ideas? Encourage the rest of the class to suggest alternatives where appropriate.	

DAY 4 ■ Writing connected prose from notes

Key features	Stages	Additional opportunities
	Introduction Ask the children to recall the purpose of notes when writing connected prose. Encourage them to discuss the need to make good, brief notes prior to writing connected prose. Why do they think a piece of writing may be unsuccessful if notes are not prepared first?	**Extend:** express opinions
Communication: use notes to write connected prose	**Speaking and listening** Begin to talk about how notes can be filled out into connected prose. Ask a volunteer to read out his or her notes from yesterday, for one paragraph, while you model how to fill them out into connected prose. On the board continue to model how to fill out the notes. Encourage the children to help you. Remind them to listen while others speak and not to interrupt.	
	Independent work Now ask the children to fill out their own brief notes into connected prose modelling their work on your demonstration. Remind them to proofread their work at the end and to check for punctuation and spelling. Give them 15 minutes to complete this task.	**Support:** proofread work for spelling and punctuation
Evaluation: give feedback	**Plenary** Choose three or four volunteers to read out first their notes and then their connected pieces of prose. Do the others agree that the connected prose relates well to the notes prepared earlier? If not, can they suggest alternatives?	

DAY 5 ■ Researching information

Key features	Stages	Additional opportunities
	Introduction Spend time talking about the work the children did yesterday. Encourage them to think about the importance of writing brief notes to support further writing in information texts.	**Phonics:** use phonic skills in writing
Self-awareness: listening skills, identify key ideas	**Speaking and listening** Discuss how they made notes on Day 3. What sort of things did they look for in a text when making notes, for example being aware of key words and sentences; abbreviating ideas and so on. Read a passage from a non-fiction text about rationing during the Second World War. Invite the children to identify key words or abbreviate ideas. Write their suggestions on the board.	**Support:** practise listening skills; concentrating on the task in hand
Communication: work collaboratively	**Independent work** Organise the children into threes and invite them to make notes on an aspect of food supplies in the Second World War that interests them. Provide books for them to research this task. Tell the children to work collaboratively with one child acting as scribe, another as leader and the third as mentor. Tell them they have 20 minutes to complete this task.	
	Plenary When the time is up, bring the class back together. Ask one group of three children to share their notes. Do the others agree that the notes will be useful for future writing? How could they be improved?	

DAY 6 ■ Using research notes in prose

Key features	Stages	Additional opportunities
	Introduction Talk about the notes taken yesterday. Remind the children how notes help us to write connected prose. Point out the importance of writing information in a logical sequence made easier if there are notes to refer to.	**Support:** give children note-taking rules
	Speaking and listening Spend time discussing the task from yesterday. Point out to the children that it was their second attempt at writing notes. Did they find it easier to make notes after the earlier practice they had on Day 3? What things did they find difficult? Did each member of the group work well in the role they had been given? Encourage all the children to participate in this discussion. Revise how notes are used as a basis for writing connected prose.	**Extend:** express opinions
	Independent work Ask the children to reform the same groups they had yesterday but to swap roles. Tell the children they are going to work collaboratively to fill out the notes they made into connected prose. Ask the leader in each group to suggest the order of writing and the style required. Ask the mentor to be prepared to advise on content, spelling and grammar. Remind the scribe to write neatly.	
Communication: work collaboratively, adopting roles	**Plenary** Invite one group to read out their work. Do they feel the connected prose reflects the order of the notes they made yesterday? Have they paid close attention to spelling and writing? Ask the class to comment.	

Guided reading and writing

Find out more about rationing. Find and read government booklets or posters about rationing and food allowances during the war. Use books and websites to research this topic. (A useful website is www.iwm.org.uk.) Talk about what the children have read. What additional information have they found out about rationing? What amounts of, for example tea and sugar, were allowed per week? Encourage the children to make notes about information they find to use in future writing.

Assessment

Provide children with appropriate books on the Second World War. Ask them to choose a subject related to children and nutrition at that time, such as children's meals in the war. Ask them to make notes independently and then to use those notes to write a piece of connected prose. Use this work to gauge the children's level of skill and understanding.

Refer back to the learning outcomes on page 119.

Further work

If difficulties emerge from the assessment activity, revisit appropriate sections of the Phase to give practice. Encourage further research by asking children to look up old recipes from the war in books or on the internet, for example for spam, dried egg.

Some of the recipes could be prepared as part of cookery lessons. Invite children to record information about how they prepared the meals and what they tasted like.

Support less confident learners by asking them to write out a recipe from the war years, reminding them to proofread their work for spelling and punctuation.

DAY 1 ▪ Information from photographs and diagrams

Key features	Stages	Additional opportunities
Self-awareness: use a visual image to glean information; respond to photographs	**Introduction** Introduce this Phase by telling the children about some of the uncomfortable things the children had to do or wear to keep themselves safe during the war. Explain, in simple terms, about Anderson shelters, Morrison shelters and gas masks. **Speaking and listening** Display the photograph of children wearing gas masks from the CD-ROM. Explain that we can get information from a variety of sources, including photographs. Discuss what the children can see of the mask and what each part is for. Ask them to express an opinion about it. Do they think it would be comfortable to wear? Why/why not? Do they think little children would have been happy to wear such things? Point out that everyone, including children, was expected to carry their masks with them all the time. **Independent work** Ask the children to draw and label a gas mask. Alternatively, they may use the interactive activity 'Gas mask' from the CD-ROM to drag and drop the correct labels into place. Remind them to check spellings if labelling the parts themselves and to read the labels carefully if using the interactive activity. **Plenary** Invite two children to show their completed work to the class. Ask the others to check that the work has been labelled correctly.	**Support:** prompt children to express opinions **Phonics:** use phonic skills when labelling

DAY 2 ▪ Using notes to recall information

Key features	Stages	Additional opportunities
Self-awareness: respond to photographs **Communication:** present information orally **Evaluation:** discuss success criteria and give feedback	**Introduction** Remind the children of yesterday's lesson. What things did they learn about the gas mask purely from studying the photograph? **Speaking and listening** Choose a non-fiction book of your choice and read an extract from it about gas masks. Before reading, remind the children to listen carefully because they will be discussing what you read. After reading, encourage the children to recall what they have heard. Take the opportunity to revisit how notes are made from texts read. **Independent work** Ask the children to make brief notes about what they have heard. Remind them to think about key words or sentences and to list abbreviations of ideas. Allow them five or six minutes to complete this activity. **Plenary** At the end of the time, call the children back together. Ask two or three children to read out their notes. Do the others think the notes are adequate? Can they suggest improvements? Re-read the extract that you read out earlier. Ask the children to proofread their own work to see if they can make any improvements.	**Extend:** expect good social skills, listening without interruption **Support:** children make notes using phonics skills for spelling

DAY 3 ■ Information through role play

Key features	Stages	Additional opportunities
	Introduction Talk about the work you did yesterday. Remind the children of the notes they made. Ask them what features they included in their notes, such as key words and sentences and abbreviated ideas.	**Support:** practise note-taking skills
Creative thinking: generate and extend imaginative ideas to explain a process; create roles	**Speaking and listening** Display the photograph of the children in gas masks from the CD-ROM. Recap on the information gleaned about it initially from studying the photograph. Point out that they can extend this information and suggest a hypothesis from using their imaginations. For example, just by examining the gas mask, they can draw conclusions about how the masks were put on and how difficult they must have been to put on because of the rubber fabric.	**Extend:** draw conclusions
Empathy: children empathise with characters from the past	**Independent work** Place the children into groups and ask them to role play a scenario in which they have to wear gas masks for a practice during the war. Ask them to choose one child to be the teacher and the others to be the pupils. Invite them to collect ideas about their role play. For example: Do they have to help each other to do up the straps? Are the masks difficult to pull on? Do they smell horrible?	
	Plenary Choose two groups of children to present their role plays. What additional information can the class glean about gas masks from watching these performances? Encourage the audience members to make notes about what they learn.	

DAY 4 ■ Prose based on several sets of notes

Key features	Stages	Additional opportunities
Evaluation: discuss role play exercise as a means of obtaining information	**Introduction** Encourage the children to recall the role play they did yesterday. Select children to read out their notes on extra information about gas masks that they gleaned from watching the role plays.	**HFWs:** put, she, he, on, it, have, had, was
	Speaking and listening Remind the children of all the different ways they have found out information about gas masks. Point out that all these sources of information are useful when preparing to write a piece of connected prose. Ask the children to discuss what they have found out using all the different sets of notes that they have been making. Encourage the children to listen and take turns.	**Extend:** recognise sources of information
Communication: work collaboratively to write a piece of prose	**Independent work** In pairs, ask the children to use their notes to develop and refine their ideas before writing connected prose on gas masks. Suggest that one child in each pair acts as scribe. Remind them also to use commas to mark clauses and apostrophes to mark possession.	**Support:** support children in taking turns
	Plenary Invite children to read out their work to the rest of the class. Ask the class to check for accuracy and to suggest alternatives where appropriate.	

DAY 5 ■ Editing written work

Key features	Stages	Additional opportunities
Evaluation: discuss and assess the value of information	### Introduction Remind the children of the pieces of connected prose they wrote yesterday. Select one or two children to read aloud their pieces. Point out that these contain some information that is less important than others. Give an example from one of the children's work.	
	### Speaking and listening Demonstrate how to edit a paragraph by deleting the less important elements, for example repetitions, asides and secondary considerations. Explain the reasons for the edits you make. Invite the children to edit a paragraph from a volunteer's work. Encourage them to give reasons for they changes they make.	
Evaluation and collaboration: children work collaboratively to edit prose	### Independent work Invite the children to re-examine their own pieces of writing, working in the same pairs as yesterday. Ask them to edit the work as demonstrated earlier in the lesson. Tell them to make notes on the reasons for their edits.	
	### Plenary At the end of the lesson, invite two or three pairs of children to read out first their unedited version and then their edited one, together with any notes justifying their edits. Examine these pieces of work with the rest of the class to highlight where edits work well and where they can be improved further to give a crisper piece of prose.	

Guided reading and writing

Recall that in Day 1 you mentioned Anderson shelters and Morrison shelters that people gathered in during the war to keep them safe from bomb explosions. Invite the children to find out more about these by reading non-fiction texts on the Second World War. Talk about what they have read. Where did people get the shelters from? How easy/difficult were they to put up?

Encourage the children to make notes on the information they find to share with the others at a later date.

Assessment

Use the CD-ROM assessment activity to assess the children's ability to edit down an extract giving reasons for their editorial choices. On completion of this task, check the children's work to assess their understanding.

Refer back to the learning outcomes on page 119.

Further work

Where difficulties arise from the assessment activity, revisit sections of the Phase to provide practice.

Extend the guided reading exercise by asking the children to write a piece of connected prose about Anderson and Morrison shelters. Take the opportunity to remind them about using commas to mark clauses and to use apostrophes for possession, where necessary.

Dictionary work

■ Put these words in alphabetical order as you would find them in a dictionary. Then write the correct definition by each word.

Words

ration	evacuee	billet	soldier	war
enemy	bomb	evacuation	blitz	invasion

Definitions:

■ Someone who was evacuated during the war.

■ The heavy bombing of a place.

■ Moving people from a dangerous place to a safer place during a war.

■ An allowance of food or clothing when such items are in short supply.

■ A place to lodge.

■ A serious fight between countries.

■ Someone who is a member of an army.

■ An opponent or foe.

■ A shell that explodes.

■ The entering of a country by an attacking army.

Word	Definition
1. _____	_____
2. _____	_____
3. _____	_____
4. _____	_____
5. _____	_____
6. _____	_____
7. _____	_____
8. _____	_____
9. _____	_____
10. _____	_____

Name _____ **Date** _____

Famous people from the Second World War

Winston Churchill

_____

_____

_____

_____

General Montgomery

_____

_____

_____

_____

Guy Gibson

_____

_____

_____

_____

General Charles de Gaulle

_____

_____

_____

_____

Winston Churchill, General Montgomery and General Charles de Gaulle photographs ©Illustrated London News; Guy Gibson: © Popperfoto/Reuters/Popperfoto.com.

NON-FICTION ■ UNIT 2

Food in the Second World War

■ Mark and annotate key words, key sentences and paragraphs.

Before the war

Before the war much of our food was brought into Britain from other countries in ships. However, when the war began this became very difficult. Many of the food-carrying ships were sunk by German submarines.

This meant that a lot of foods became scarce.

Rationing

Because foods became scarce, they had to be rationed. Rationing means that food is shared out in a fair way so that everyone has the same amount. The government decided that the fairest way to make sure everyone got the same amount of food was to give each person their own ration book. The ration books had coupons in them. If someone bought a rationed item of food a coupon was torn out of the ration book. That way, no one could have more than their fair share.

Some people were allowed extra rations. Children under five years of age were given extra rations.

Text © 2007, Sue Graves.

NON-FICTION
UNIT 3 Explanation texts

Speak and listen for a range of purposes on paper and on screen

Strand 1 Speaking
- Respond appropriately to the contributions of others in the light of differing viewpoints.

Strand 2 Listening and responding
- Identify how talk varies with age, familiarity, gender and purpose.

Read for a range of purposes on paper and on screen

Strand 7 Understanding and interpreting texts
- Deduce characters' reasons for behaviour from their actions and explain how ideas are developed in non-fiction texts.
- Use knowledge of different organisational features of texts to find information effectively.

Strand 8 Engaging with and responding to texts
- Read extensively favourite authors or genres and experiment with other types of text.
- Interrogate texts to deepen and clarify understanding and response.

Write for a range of purposes on paper and on screen

Strand 9 Creating and shaping texts
- Develop and refine ideas in writing using planning, problem-solving strategies.
- Summarise and shape material and ideas from different sources to write convincing and informative non-narrative texts.

Strand 10 Text structure and organisation
- Organise texts into paragraphs to distinguish between different information, events or processes.
- Use adverbs and conjunctions to establish cohesion within paragraphs.

Strand 11 Sentence structure and punctuation
- Clarify meaning and point of view by using varied sentence structure (phrases, clauses and adverbials).
- Use commas to mark clauses and the apostrophe for possession.

Strand 12 Presentation
- Use word-processing packages to present written work and continue to increase speed and accuracy in typing.

Progression in explanation texts

In this year children are moving towards:
- Reading and analysing explanatory texts to identify key features.
- Distinguishing between explanatory texts, reports and recount while recognising that an information book might contain examples of all these.
- Summarising processes carried out in the classroom and on screen in flow charts or cyclical diagrams.
- Using paragraphs, connectives and other key language and structural features when writing an explanation.
- Writing explanatory texts from a flow chart or other diagrammatic plan, using the conventions modelled in shared writing.

▶

UNIT 3 ◄ Explanation texts continued

Key aspects of learning covered in this Unit

Enquiry
Children will ask questions arising from viewing a short film. They will investigate a range of texts, research and then plan how to present information effectively.

Creative thinking
Children will generate and extend imaginative ideas to explain a process. They will suggest hypotheses, responding imaginatively through drama and talk, and respond to problems in order to create a written outcome.

Information processing
Children will identify relevant information from a range of sources on paper and on screen and use this to write their own explanation texts.

Reasoning
Children will use different sources to develop the language of cause and effect. They will draw inferences and conclusions to clarify, extend and follow up ideas in their oral and written work.

Evaluation
Children will present information orally, diagrammatically and in writing. They will discuss success criteria, give feedback to others and judge effectiveness of their own work.

Communication
Children will develop their ability to explain a process orally. They will learn how to locate information in different types of text and how to present written information in a particular form.

Prior learning

Before starting this Unit check that the children can:
■ Identify the key features of simple recount and report texts.
■ Express clear opinions about characters' responses to a range of settings.
■ Navigate information texts on paper and on screen using knowledge of text type and layout to identify facts and points of interest.
If they need further support please refer to a prior Unit or a similar Unit in Year 3.

Resources

Phase 1:
Popular plastic by Sue Graves ❀; Non-fiction books on the environment and recycling; Interactive activity 'Recycling newspaper' ❀; Photocopiable page 145 'Paper recycling'
Phase 2:
Non-fiction books on recycling, such as *Trash to Treasure* by Sue Graves (HarperCollins); Voice recorders; Word-processing software; Film clip showing a recycling process; Photocopiable page 146 'Letter writing'
Phase 3:
Recycling machine illustration ❀; Explanation texts on recycling and other explanation texts such as *The Way Things Work* by Chris Oxlade and Michael Harris (Lorenz Books); Word-processing software; Photocopiable page 147 'The recycling machine'; Photocopiable page 148 'All about the recycling machine'; Assessment illustration: Recycling garden ❀

Cross-curricular opportunities

Geography and PSHE – The environment

UNIT 3 ■ Teaching sequence

Phase	Children's objectives	Summary of activities	Learning outcomes
1	I can read and discuss different text types. I can identify and discuss key features of explanatory texts. I understand the importance of punctuation and word order. I can reorder a text so it is easier to understand. I can write explanatory labels for a diagram.	Examine features of recounts, reports and explanatory texts. Mark key features of explanatory text. Annotate key features of explanatory texts. Analyse grammar, punctuation, word order. Create an explanatory diagram.	Children can compare and contrast non-fiction text types. Children can identify key features and use this knowledge to find information quickly. Children understand the importance of grammar, punctuation and word order to support meaning and how ideas are developed in an explanation text. Children can summarise explanations using diagrams.
2	I can listen to and discuss oral explanations. I can write an explanatory letter. I can analyse an explanatory film and then role play one of the characters. I can work with others to plan a film sequence still.	Record oral explanations. Write explanatory text (letter). Role play part of a process. Suggest appropriate film stills.	Children can recognise structure and language features in oral explanations. Children can explain an answer to a question using language features of the text type. Children can explain a process using role play. Children can explain a process visually.
3	I can examine and discuss information from visual sources. I can use labels and a flow chart to explain a process. I can work with others to produce oral and written explanations. I can proofread and edit written work.	Label a diagram. Label and discuss a process. Give oral explanations. Rehearse and practise sentences. Prepare rough draft collaboratively. Edit work to produce final explanation piece.	Children can obtain information from an oral source and use it as a basis for explanation. Children can use information collected from more than one source, including a diagrammatic plan, and present it in the form of an explanation text using genre conventions. Children can appraise the appropriateness of edits in final drafts.

Provide copies of the objectives for the children.

DAY 1 ▌ Recounts, reports and explanation features

Key features	Stages	Additional opportunities
	Introduction To introduce this topic ask the children to recall the features of a report and a recount text. Encourage all the children to contribute. Tell them that in this Unit they are going to investigate explanation texts	**Phonics:** split unfamiliar words into phonemes for reading **HFWs:** read on sight: at, the, after, next **MFWs:** during
Creative thinking: explain a process	**Speaking and listening** Display and read *Popular plastic* from the CD-ROM. After reading spend time discussing its contents, take the opportunity to talk about the importance of recycling to help the environment. Point out the features of this explanation text. Use key questions to help children locate these features, such as *What is the purpose of the extract?* Make a list of their remarks on the board. Select children to recount orally how they recycle plastic at home. How does a recount differ from an explanation text?	
Communication: working collaboratively	**Independent work** In pairs, invite the children to read a report about recycling from the Internet, perhaps a county council report on its recycling. How does a report differ from an explanation text? Ask them to discuss this fully and make notes if needed. Allow them 20 minutes to do this task.	
	Plenary Bring the children back together. Ask them to distinguish between explanatory texts, recounts and reports, giving examples from what they have read or heard.	

DAY 2 ▌ Key features of explanation texts

Key features	Stages	Additional opportunities
	Introduction Remind the children of the work they did yesterday on explanatory texts. Ask them to recall the features of this text type. Remind the children to take turns and not call out.	**Phonics:** split difficult words into phonemes for reading. **Support:** practise turn-taking
	Speaking and listening Display *Popular plastic* from the CD-ROM. Re-read the extract together. Discuss the key features of this text. For example, ask the children to find the aim of the piece (to explain a purpose). Encourage all the children to participate fully and to give their reasons for suggestions that they make.	
Information processing: identify relevant information	**Independent work** Print copies of the extract, one per pair of children. Ask the pairs to discuss the extract together and then to mark it to identify key features, of purpose, structure, language and presentation. Allow them 15 minutes to complete this task.	
Evaluation: present reasons orally	**Plenary** When the time is up, ask for volunteers to share their work with the class. Ask them to explain their selections of key features and to justify their decisions. Do the others agree with the choices made? What other suggestions can they make?	**Extend:** justify decisions

DAY 3 ■ Finding information in explanation texts

Key features	Stages	Additional opportunities
	Introduction Spend time reminding the children of the work you did yesterday and how they identified the key features of an explanatory text. Tell them that they are going to revisit the text to annotate and highlight its key features.	**Support:** children identify key features
Information processing and evaluation: identify relevant information	**Speaking and listening** Display *Popular plastic* from the CD-ROM and highlight and annotate the key features of the explanatory text. Encourage the children to make suggestions to help you do this. Then talk about the list of features you and the children have identified. Encourage the children to find information quickly using their knowledge of these organisational features.	**Support:** children express opinions, make suggestions
	Independent work Provide the children with explanatory texts about recycling on screen or on paper. Ask them to use on-screen tools or writing materials, as appropriate, to mark up the extract to highlight and annotate the key features of an explanatory text. Allow them 20 minutes to complete this task.	
Communication: present information orally	**Plenary** Invite several children to share their work. Ask them to make comparisons of the texts they have examined and their features. On the board make a list of the features of an explanatory text the children have identified to use throughout the teaching sequence.	**Extend:** provide feedback on work

DAY 4 ■ Word order and punctuation

Key features	Stages	Additional opportunities
	Introduction Ask the children what they remember from the previous day's lesson. Select children to recall the features of an explanatory text.	
	Speaking and listening Display *Popular plastic* from the CD-ROM. Invite a child to read the extract to the class. Take the opportunity to draw attention to the way commas, connectives and full stops are used to join and separate clauses. Talk about the importance of word order. Why is it important and how does it affect meaning? Invite the children to experiment with changing word order to see how meaning is affected. Extend the above by discussing how ideas are developed in an explanation text.	**Support:** provide children with grammar and punctuation terms
Communication: working collaboratively; explain a process orally	**Independent work** Ask the children to work in groups of three or four. Tell them to choose a short explanation extract from a book on the environment and discuss the uses of commas, connectives and full stops to join and separate clauses. Ask them to find examples where meaning is changed if word order is altered.	**Extend:** children apply grammar and punctuation skills
	Plenary Ask for volunteers to read out their group's extract and talk about what they discovered about the uses of commas, connectives and full stops. Look for examples where meaning is affected if word order is changed.	

DAY 5 ▪ Using diagrams to clarify an explanation

Key features	Stages	Additional opportunities
	### Introduction Remind the children of the work they have done so far on explanation texts. Use prompt questions to stimulate recall of the critical features of an explanation text.	**HFWs:** spell: first, next, then, after, that **Extend:** justify decisions
	### Speaking and listening Display the interactive activity 'Recycling newspaper' from the CD-ROM. It contains an explanation that has been given in the wrong order. Together read the extract as it stands. Discuss it in its present form. Is it easy to work out the recycling process? Why not? Invite the children to help you put the extract into the right order. Use prompt questions to guide them: *Which part of the explanation will come first? What clues are there to justify and support our views?* The diagram will help them.	
Creative thinking: use labels to explain a process	### Independent work Provide each child with a copy of photocopiable page 145 'Paper recycling'. Ask the children to write explanatory labels alongside each part of the paper recycling process. Allow them 10 minutes to complete this task.	
Evaluation: discuss success criteria and give feedback	### Plenary Ask three children to show their work to the others. Invite the rest of the class to check for accuracy and to offer alternatives where appropriate. Point out that diagrams such as these support clarity of explanations.	**Support:** clarify explanations

Guided reading

Use non-fiction texts on recycling or improving the environment to provide further practice of explanation texts. Spend time talking about the books. Did the book have a mixture of text types? How could the children tell? Ask them to identify key features of explanations, recounts and reports to compare and contrast these text types.

Assessment

During introductions and the speaking and listening sections of the Phase, check that all the children are participating fully in the lessons. Take the opportunity to make an oral assessment to see if the children understand and recall the features of explanatory texts. Provide explanation texts and ask the children to identify key features from them.

Refer back to the learning outcomes on page 135.

Further work

Where difficulties arise in the assessment activity, provide extra work in that area to support learning.

For further work, invite the children to use the internet or local newspapers to find out about recycling in the area. Encourage them to find examples of explanation texts on this subject where diagrams support clarity.

Support children to read a diagram to work out a simple recycling process.

DAY 1 ■ Oral explanations

Key features	Stages	Additional opportunities
	### Introduction Introduce this Phase by outlining the following scenario. Tell the children that you are the manager of a paper mill and that the machinery at the mill has broken down. This means that the recycling lorry cannot collect everyone's waste paper this week. Ensure when you give this explanation to the class that you include all the features of an explanation text: purpose, structure, language features and so on.	
	### Speaking and listening Invite the children to talk about what they have heard. Ask them to break down the oral explanation to reveal the language features mentioned in the introduction above. Encourage the children to take turns to speak and not to interrupt while others are speaking. Make notes of their observations on the board.	**Support:** listen while others speak without interrupting
Communication: explain a process orally	### Independent work Put children into groups and ask them to record simple explanations about other recycling processes. Many of these can be found in *Trash to Treasure* by Sue Graves. Remind them to use explanation language features when speaking.	**Extend** give oral explanations
Evaluation: discuss success criteria	### Plenary Select one or two groups to play their recordings to the others. Ask the groups to identify language features, in their oral explanations. Do the others agree that the oral explanations meet the criteria of explanation texts? What suggestions can they make to improve them?	

DAY 2 ■ Explanatory letters

Key features	Stages	Additional opportunities
	### Introduction Recall the paper mill manager's oral explanation from yesterday. Take the opportunity to revise key features of an oral explanation.	**HFWs:** because, so **Support:** help children to identify key features
Information processing: write a letter as a group	### Speaking and listening Tell the children that the manager would have to write to tell the people why their waste paper cannot be collected this week. Ask the children to help you write an explanatory letter on the board. Take the opportunity to remind the children of the conventions of letter-writing. Together read the completed letter. Check that it meets the criteria for this text type.	
Reasoning: write a letter	### Independent work Let the children write their own explanatory letters on screen or paper. Ask them to think of different explanations why the paper mill cannot recycle papers next week. Allow them 20 minutes to write their letters. If wished, children may use photocopiable page 146 'Letter writing' to help them write their letters.	**Extend:** improve word-processing skills
	### Plenary Invite three or four children to read out their explanations. Ask the other children to check that the explanations meet the criteria for this text type. Invite them to suggest alternatives where appropriate.	

DAY 3 ■ Dramatic explanations

Key features	Stages	Additional opportunities
	Introduction Talk about the work the children have done over the last two days. Encourage them to recall the features of explanatory texts.	
Social skills: watch without speaking or interrupting	**Speaking and listening** Show a film about a recycling process, such as waste paper being taken to a paper mill for recycling. After watching the film, discuss it with the children. Ask them to identify the sequence of the process and the people involved.	
Communication: give an oral explanation using role play	**Independent work** Invite the children to give an oral explanation of the recycling process using role play. Organise the children into groups and ask them to choose to be, for example, the lorry driver, the manager of the mill or the people working on each of the recycling sections. Allow them 20 minutes to practise their role plays.	
Evaluation: assess performances	**Plenary** Select a group of children to present their role play. Invite the others to assess performances including the adequacy of the oral explanations.	

DAY 4 ■ Explanation

Key features	Stages	Additional opportunities
	Introduction Talk about how, in their roles, the children explained the recycling process.	**Support:** recall features of oral explanations
	Speaking and listening Re-watch the film you saw yesterday about recycling. Talk about the way the film is sequenced to explain a process. Explain that a shot in a film can be frozen to make a 'still'. Demonstrate how choose stills to show part of the recycling process.	**Extend:** use extended vocabulary to discuss the film
	Independent work Put the children into pairs and ask them to plan a sequence of stills from the film to show the process of recycling. Allow 20 minutes for this task.	
Communication: work collaboratively to choose stills to explain a process	**Plenary** Choose one pair to present their plans to the others. Do the others agree that the planned stills identify distinct parts of the process?	

Guided reading
Provide the children with an explanation text on recycling. Ask them to identify key features: purpose, structure, language features. After reading, encourage the children to give oral explanations in response to prompts from you, such as *What happens first?*

Assessment
During whole class teaching, assess the children's understanding by asking them to give oral explanations about a recycling process of their choice. Remind them to use language features of explanation texts such as: *first... then... next.*
Refer back to the learning outcomes on page 135.

Further work
Ask the children to examine other recycling processes and write explanation texts about them. Remind them to organise their explanations sequentially and to use language features of this text type.

DAY 1 ▪ Using labels to provide information

Key features	Stages	Additional opportunities
	Introduction Talk about the work done in Phase 2 about explanations (recycling processes). Ask the children to recall, for example, how paper is recycled. Encourage all the children to participate.	
Creative thinking: investigate the workings of an imaginary machine; write labels	**Speaking and listening** Display the illustration from the CD-ROM showing an imaginary machine that can be fitted into every home and which can recycle everything! Spend time examining the machine and discussing how useful it might be and how the children think it works. Remind the children to take turns to speak and to listen when others are talking.	**Extend:** use wider vocabulary to explain a process
	Independent work Provide the children with copies of Photocopiable page 147 'The recycling machine'. Ask them to write labels to identify as many parts of the machine as they can. Tell them to complete the task in ten minutes.	
Reasoning: draw inferences **Evaluating:** express opinions	**Plenary** Select children to read their labels aloud to the others. How will the labels help them when they are writing their explanations about this machine, at a later date? Having examined the machine in this way, do they think that an item such as this would make people recycle more conscientiously? Why? Why not?	

DAY 2 ▪ Using a flow chart to provide information

Key features	Stages	Additional opportunities
	Introduction Remind the children of the work they did yesterday. You could, invite two or three children to read aloud the notes they made on the machine. Spend time discussing the usefulness of the machine.	**Extend:** express an opinion
	Speaking and listening Display the illustration from the CD-ROM. Use the highlighter tool, to demonstrate how to select interesting parts of the machine. Ask the children to consider what these parts might be for and how they might work. Encourage all the children to express an opinion but to wait their turn while others are speaking.	**Support:** listen and evaluate another's point of view
Communication: work collaboratively	**Independent work** Organise the children into pairs and ask them to create a detailed diagram of their chosen part of the machine. Tell them to label and discuss together how they think this part of the machine works. (This oral rehearsal will act as a structure to support future writing on Day 6). Allow the children ten minutes for this activity.	
Evaluation: give reasons for choices; appraise peers' work	**Plenary** At the end of the allowed time, bring the children back together. Invite three or four pairs to discuss their findings with the class. Find out how many other pairs of children focused on the same part of the machine. What other sections were chosen? Ask the children to give reasons for their choices.	

DAY 3 ◼ Using visual information

Key features	Stages	Additional opportunities
	Introduction Talk about the work you did yesterday. Ask the children to recall how interesting sections of the machine were highlighted on screen. Ask a child to demonstrate the process. Invite the others to make suggestions as appropriate.	
Creative thinking: explain a process	**Speaking and listening** Provide the children with copies of the recycling machine illustration and gather ideas on technical names for particular parts of the machine, for example the waste-sorter. Invite the children to discuss how this part of the machine might work. How, for example, can it detect different types of waste? Encourage all the children to participate, they could annotate the image or just discuss the different aspects.	**Extend:** use extended vocabulary to devise technical names
Reasoning and communication: work collaboratively and give oral explanations	**Independent work** In small groups ask the children to discuss different sections of the machine. Encourage them to agree on a simple explanation about how one part of the machine works. Ask them to elect a spokesperson to give an oral explanation during the plenary. Allow the children 20 minutes for this task.	
	Plenary Call the children back together. Ask the spokespeople from the groups to take turns to give their oral explanations. Take the opportunity to recap on the features of an explanation, such as its purpose and structure.	**Support:** revisit features of an explanation

DAY 4 ◼ Practising explanatory sentences

Key features	Stages	Additional opportunities
	Introduction Point out that over the last three days the children have been using a visual image as the basis for constructing an oral explanation. Refer the children back to the explanation texts they examined in Phase 1 of this Unit. Can they recall the features of an explanation text?	**Phonics:** look at the vowel phoneme *or*
Creative thinking: explain a purpose and process	**Speaking and listening** Display the imaginary recycling machine from the CD-ROM. Recalling previous work on explanation texts, ask the children to suggest good sentences to explain the purpose of the machine. Encourage the children to participate fully, but to listen without interrupting while others are speaking.	**Support:** revisit earlier work
	Independent work Using their individual whiteboards, ask the children to choose one part of the machine to explain how it works, bearing in mind the language conventions of an explanatory text. Allow them 15 minutes for this task. Remind them to write in complete sentences and to use correct punctuation.	
Evaluation: give feedback	**Plenary** At the end of the allotted time, invite four children to read their work to the others. Do the others agree that the sentences meet the criteria for explanation texts? Can they be improved? Take the opportunity to check for good sentence structure and punctuation.	

DAY 5 ■ Drafting an explanation text

Key features	Stages	Additional opportunities
	Introduction Read the children a short explanatory text about recycling. After reading ask the children to recall the contents of the extract in their own words.	**HFWs:** first, then, next, after that
Enquiry and evaluation: discuss the effectiveness of a new explanation text	**Speaking and listening** Together identify success criteria for the extract you read out. Does it meet the criteria of an explanatory text? Can the children identify purpose, structure? What language features can they see? Ask them to notice paragraphs and their purpose in breaking up the text into logical steps to aid the explanation process. Encourage the children to participate fully in this discussion. Discuss how to write an explanation text about the recycling machine illustrated on the CD-ROM. Encourage the children to refer to visual planning aids; notes and so on from earlier sessions.	**Support:** encourage children to identify criteria of explanatory text
Communication: use information collected from more than one source	**Independent work** Put the children into pairs. Ask the children to work on a rough draft of an explanation text of how the machine works based on earlier discussions and referring to visual planning aids, diagrams and notes. Invite one child in each pair to act as scribe. Allow them 15 minutes to complete this task.	
	Plenary When the time is up, choose three or four 'scribes' to read their work to the others. Encourage the rest of the children to listen carefully to what is read and to offer suggestions for improvements.	

DAY 6 ■ Editing to produce a final piece of writing

Key features	Stages	Additional opportunities
	Introduction Talk about the work the children did yesterday. Point out that they prepared their rough drafts using information collected from more than one source. Ask them to identify the sources they used, such as visual planning aids and notes.	**HFWs:** connectives: and, but, because, so
Evaluation: identify success criteria	**Speaking and listening** Revisit the success criteria for writing an explanatory text. List the criteria on the board. Ask for a volunteer to read out his/her rough draft from yesterday. Discuss how the work could be made more cohesive, for example by using appropriate connectives. Rewrite the piece of writing on the board to demonstrate how the edits make the piece more cohesive.	**Support:** help children use connectives appropriately
Information processing: write and edit	**Independent work** Tell the children to work in the same pairs as yesterday. Ask them to edit their writing into final pieces of work, using connectives to make their writing more cohesive. Allow them 20 minutes for this task. Some children could write their final piece on photocopiable page 148 'About the recycling machine' if support is needed.	
	Plenary Choose three pairs of children to share their work with the class. Ask them to self-appraise their final pieces. Do the others agree with these appraisals? If not, why not? Have they met the success criteria in their writing as discussed earlier in the lesson?	

Guided reading

Read other explanation texts with the children, for example *The Way Things Work* by Chris Oxlade and Michael Harris. Does the book meet the criteria of an explanation text? How do paragraphs aid sequencing of an explanation? Ask the children to find examples in the text to support their answers to your questions.

Assessment

Look at the stimulus image from the CD-ROM showing a garden which is using a lot of recycling. Ask children to Write an explanation about how things can be recycled to be used in a garden.

Encourage them to use word banks, visual planning aids and notes to help them write this piece. Remind them to use good sentence structure and to proofread their finished pieces for spelling and grammar.

Check the children's work to ensure they have met the success criteria for writing that you have discussed in this Unit. Refer back to the learning outcomes on page 135.

Further work

Invite the children to work on their presentation skills.

Discuss how an explanation may have to be adjusted to suit the intended audience. For example, what things would they consider when presenting an explanation to a Key Stage 1 audience as opposed to Key Stage 2?

Encourage the children to word-process their final drafts. Suggest they use and label images from the CD-ROM or draw their own diagrams to insert into their work. Their finished work can be presented as an electronic or paper-based book.

Name _____ **Date** _____

Paper recycling

■ Write the labels in the correct boxes to complete the diagram about paper recycling.

Ink, staples and paper clips are removed.	The old newspapers are taken to the paper mill in a lorry.	The pulp is sprayed on to mesh screens.
The old papers are mixed with water.	The old newspapers are tied up into bales.	The pulp is dried, pressed and rolled into new sheets of paper.

Illustrations © Peter Lubach / Beehive Illustration.

Letter writing

(Write your address here)

———————————————————

———————————————————

———————————————————

———————————————————

(Write the date here)

———————————————————

Dear ————————————————————

(Apologise that waste paper will not be collected next week)

————————————————————————————

————————————————————————————

————————————————————————————

————————————————————————————

————————————————————————————

(Explain why it won't be collected)

————————————————————————————

————————————————————————————

————————————————————————————

————————————————————————————

————————————————————————————

Yours faithfully,

———————————————————

(Write your name here)

100 LITERACY FRAMEWORK LESSONS YEAR 4

PHOTOCOPIABLE

■SCHOLASTIC
www.scholastic.co.uk

Name _____   **Date** _____

The recycling machine

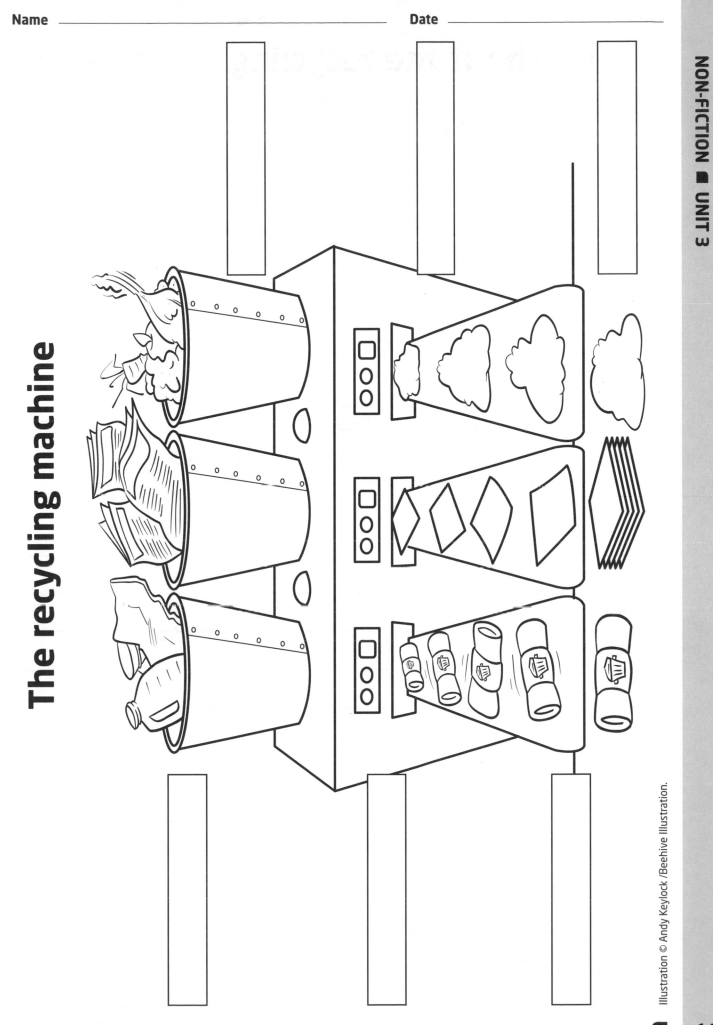

NON-FICTION ■ UNIT 3

All about the recycling machine

■ Write sentences to explain what the recycling machine is and how it works.

■ What the recycling machine is:

_____

_____

_____

_____

_____

_____

■ This is how it works:

_____

_____

_____

_____

_____

_____

Illustration © Andy Keylock /Beehive Illustration.

■ 100 LITERACY FRAMEWORK LESSONS YEAR 4

PHOTOCOPIABLE ■SCHOLASTIC
www.scholastic.co.uk

NON-FICTION
UNIT 4 Persuasive texts

Speak and listen for a range of purposes on paper and on screen

Strand 1 Speaking
- Respond appropriately to the contributions of others in light of differing viewpoints.

Strand 2 Listening and responding
- Compare the different contributions of music, words and images in short extracts from TV programmes.
- Identify how talk varies with age, familiarity, gender and purpose.

Read for a range of purposes on paper and on screen

Strand 7 Understanding and interpreting texts
- Explain how writers use figurative and expressive language to create images and atmosphere.

Strand 8 Engaging and responding to texts
- Interrogate texts to deepen and clarify understanding and response.

Write for a range of purposes on paper and on screen

Strand 9 Creating and shaping texts
- Develop and refine ideas in writing using planning and problem-solving strategies.
- Summarise and shape material and ideas from different sources to write convincing and informative non-narrative texts.
- Show imagination through language used to create emphasis, humour, atmosphere or suspense.
- Choose and combine words, images and other features for particular effects.

Strand 11 Sentence structure and punctuation
- Clarify meaning and point of view by using varied sentence structure (phrases, clauses and adverbials).

Strand 12 Presentation
- Use word-processing packages to present work and continue to increase speed and accuracy in typing.

Progression in persuasive texts

In this year children are moving towards:
- Reading, comparing and contrasting a range of paper-based and DVD-based persuasive texts; discussing and record common features of the text types; expressing views about the persuasive nature of different texts.
- Identifying elements of a DVD text that would persuade a reader to see a film; planning a trailer to promote a film using key moments from the film.
- Preparing a written voice-over script to persuade a reader to see a film. Demonstrate how to combine words, music, and images to convince the reader.

UNIT 4 ◀ **Persuasive texts** *continued*

Key aspects of learning covered in this Unit

Information processing
Children locate and refer to relevant examples from a DVD text.

Reasoning
Children will be able to give reasons for their opinions about the impact of a range of persuasive texts.

Evaluation
Children will develop their own assessment criteria to evaluate persuasive texts. They will use these when reviewing their own work and the work of others.

Social skills
When working collaboratively, children will listen to and respect other people's ideas and take on a variety of roles in a group.

Communication
Children will develop their ability to discuss as they work collaboratively in pairs, groups and whole-class contexts. They will communicate persuasively orally, in writing and through ICT if appropriate.

Prior learning

Before starting this Unit check that the children can:
■ Express opinions about a text supported with evidence from the text.
■ Write a simple sentence correctly demarcated by a capital letter and a full stop.
If they need further support please refer to a prior Unit or a similar Unit in Year 3.

Resources

Phase 1:
Range of paper-based persuasive texts discussing habitat loss and other environmental issues; *Save Our Birds!* (including differentiated version) by Sue Graves ❧; Polar bear film ❧; Similar trailers or clips (including from wildlife films); Access to www.rspb.org.uk; Photocopiable page 163 'Advertisement'; Photocopiable page 164 'Emotional response'

Phase 2:
DVD of *Watership Down*; Photocopiable page 165 'Persuasive and non-persuasive trailers'

Phase 3:
DVD of *Watership Down*; Voice-recording and image-editing software; Photocopiable page 166 'Trailer information'; Assessment activity 'Film trailers' ❧

Cross-curricular opportunities

Science – Habitats
PSHE and Citizenship – Animals and humans

UNIT 4 ■ Teaching sequence

Phase	Children's objectives	Summary of activities	Learning outcomes
1	I can discuss and annotate a persuasive text. I can identify the key features of a persuasive text. I can discuss a film trailer and analyse its features. I can compare the features of a trailer with other persuasive texts. I can evaluate and grade a trailer's persuasiveness.	Annotate visual and written text. Unpick key features of persuasive text type. Make comparisons. Work collaboratively in jigsaw groups. Work collaboratively to analyse a trailer. Work in pairs; write notes. Make comparisons.	Children can express personal opinions. Children can compare and contrast a range of texts using evidence from the texts to support their opinions.
2	I can identify key persuasive features in a film. I can select key features and make notes on them. I can discuss my choices with others and justify them. I can listen to others and offer suggestions and opinions. I can check key features of persuasive texts are present in my own work.	Write notes on persuasive features. Select features, write notes. Record key moments of a film in note form. Grade key moments in order of effectiveness. Work collaboratively; justify choices. Organise notes on key moments and plan own trailers. Check own plans.	Children can identify key persuasive features in a film. Children can select the most effective persuasive features in a film and write notes on them. Children can work collaboratively to plan an imaginary film trailer.
3	I can discuss and select key features of a film trailer. I can work in a group and make suggestions. I can listen to instructions. I can discuss the effects of emphasising different words in a voice-over. I can discuss and evaluate work done.	Identify and select features. Work collaboratively; write voice-over scripts. Write notes. Scan drawings/images. Make notes. Add voice-overs, sound effects and music.	Children can use key features in persuasive texts to create own multi-sensory persuasive presentation. Children can present the final draft of an imaginary film trailer containing the key features of a persuasive text. Children can evaluate the effectiveness of their work.

Provide copies of the objectives for the children.

DAY 1 ▪ Examining persuasive texts

Key features	Stages	Additional opportunities
	Introduction During shared reading, look at paper-based persuasive texts, including posters for films, and adverts in magazines and newspapers focusing on information about the loss of animal habitats through climate change, human intervention and so on. Discuss the purpose of the texts and how they are intended to make the reader feel, angry, worried and so on.	
	Speaking and listening Display *Save Our Birds!* from the CD-ROM. It is a poster about the effects of climate change on bird habitats (particularly nature reserves). Read the poster together. Spend time discussing its contents. Invite the children to express their opinions about the emotions the poster provokes, for example worry, pity. Annotate the poster by circling or underlining the features (both pictorial and written) identified by the children. Record the findings on the board.	**Support:** Children use the differentiated version of *Save Our Birds!*
	Independent work Hand out copies of photocopiable page 163 'Advertisement' showing an advert by a local bird-support group. Ask the children to mark and annotate features (both pictorial and written) that provoke emotion.	**Extend:** interrogate text to deepen and clarify meaning and response; justify choices
Reasoning: give reasons for their opinions	**Plenary** Analyse some of the children's work. Did everyone choose the same features? Did anyone make different choices? Ask them to give reasons for their choices.	

DAY 2 ▪ Unpicking key features

Key features	Stages	Additional opportunities
	Introduction Remind the children of the work they did yesterday. Ask them to recall the purpose of a persuasive text. Encourage all the children to participate.	
	Speaking and listening Return to the shared texts by looking at *Save Our Birds!* from the CD-ROM and by asking the children to re-examine their completed copies of photocopiable page 163 'Advertisement'. Together unpick the key features of the text structure. Make a note of the children's findings on the board.	
Social skills: work collaboratively; listen to and respect others' ideas; take on role within group	**Independent work** Put the children into groups and provide them with a selection of persuasive texts related to the subject matter addressed in Day 1. Ask them to read and discuss the texts and identify their key features. Remind them to take turns in the group and to listen to and respect other people's opinions. Ask the groups to nominate a spokesperson who will report each group's findings in the plenary.	
	Plenary At the end of the session, bring the children back together. Ask the spokespeople to report their findings on the texts read by their groups. Did all the texts conform to the same conventions that were identified in the shared session? Take the opportunity to list these conventions on the board as a reminder for further work on this text type.	**Support:** list conventions of text type

DAY 3 ■ Comparing persuasive texts

Key features	Stages	Additional opportunities
	Introduction Spend time talking about the work you did yesterday with the children. Ask them to recall the key features of a persuasive text. Remind the children to take turns and not to call out.	
	Speaking and listening Revisit the notes that linked with the *Save Our Birds!* poster from the CD-ROM. Revise the structure of paper-based persuasive texts. Encourage the children to identify the text's purpose and its key features. Point out that you are going to test these key features to see if they apply to a film trailer. Display the Polar bear film from the CD-ROM. Discuss the purpose of the trailer and the emotions it is intended to provoke in the listener. Spend time discussing the film and its similarities with the poster and advertisement texts.	**Extend:** use appropriate vocabulary and speak in sentences to make comments
Social skills: work collaboratively; listen to and respect others' ideas; take on roles within a group	**Independent work** Put the children into groups. Ask them to compare the trailer with the poster and the advertisement texts. Do they think that they all provoke the same response? Encourage them to participate fully in this discussion. Invite one child to act as scribe to record the group's findings in note form.	
	Plenary At the end of the session, ask the scribes to make a report of their group's findings using their notes as reference. Did everyone have similar findings?	**Support:** use notes for reference

DAY 4 ■ Analysing trailer components

Key features	Stages	Additional opportunities
	Introduction Talk about the work done over the last three days. Ask the children to recall the features of a persuasive text and the different types of persuasive texts they have seen and read.	**Support:** review earlier work to secure information
	Speaking and listening Re-watch the film trailer from the CD-ROM. Together identify its different components: soundtrack, voice-over and moving images. Discuss the importance of each of these features in making up the whole trailer.	
	Independent work Divide the class into two sets of two 'jigsaw' groups. Ask each group to discuss one of the trailer components (voice-over and moving images) and how it is used to persuade us to see the film. Allow them 15 minutes for this task.	
Social skills: work collaboratively; listen to and respect others' ideas; take on roles within a group	**Plenary** When the time is up, bring the groups back together. Invite the groups to share their findings. Remind the children to take turns while others in their group are speaking. Make notes about the groups findings on the board. At the end of the discussion, sum up the children's findings referring to the notes on the board as support.	

DAY 5 ▪ Evidence of persuasive devices

Key features	Stages	Additional opportunities
	Introduction Recall the previous day's lesson. Ask the children to tell you what contributions each of the components of the trailer played in persuading them to watch the complete film. Encourage reluctant participators to contribute to this section of the lesson.	**Support:** focus on reluctant participators
Information processing: use pause button on control panel	**Speaking and listening** Re-open the film clip from the CD-ROM. Model how to use the pause button on the control panel of the playback software to watch and discuss one section of the trailer. Highlight evidence of how the moving images and the sound act as persuasive devices. Encourage the children to express their opinions throughout this section. Make a note of their findings on the board.	**Extend:** use appropriate vocabulary to express opinion
Social skills: work collaboratively; listen to and respect others' ideas; take on roles within a group	**Independent work** Working in small groups, invite the children to analyse the rest of the trailer in a similar way. Encourage them to make notes of their findings and to elect a child to act as scribe to write the notes. Allow them 15 minutes for this activity.	
Evaluation: review work using own assessment criteria	**Plenary** When the time is up, bring the children back together. Ask for volunteers from each group to present their findings to the class using their notes for reference and giving examples to justify their comments. Invite the rest of the class to listen carefully and to question findings as appropriate.	**Extend:** justify comments with evidence

DAY 6 ▪ Pausing selections

Key features	Stages	Additional opportunities
	Introduction Revisit the work the children did yesterday. Invite the children to tell you how they evaluated the importance of the soundtrack and the moving images in judging how a trailer persuaded a viewer to watch a film.	**HFWs:** read/spell: good, make, made, will **MFWs:** does, don't **Support:** review earlier work
Information processing: use pause button	**Speaking and listening** Select another trailer of a wildlife film (copyright permitting) that focuses on disappearing habitats. Repeat the process from yesterday, but this time, ask the children to model how to use the pause button to view one section of the trailer. Invite the children to highlight evidence on how moving images and the soundtrack act as persuasive devices. Throughout this discussion, remind the children to take turns and respect other people's opinions even if they differ from their own.	
Social skills: work collaboratively; listen to and respect others' ideas	**Independent work** Put the children into pairs and ask them to repeat the process outlined in Speaking and listening above with a range of trailers (copyright permitting) that you have selected for this purpose and loaded onto computers. Ask one child from each pair to make notes about their findings to share with the others during the plenary. Allow 20 minutes for this activity.	**Support:** children use phonic skills for writing notes
Evaluation: review work using own assessment criteria	**Plenary** When the time is up, bring the children together. Ask one child from each pair to deliver their findings. Invite the others to discuss the findings.	

DAY 7 ■ Evaluating and grading trailers

Key features	Stages	Additional opportunities
	### Introduction This is the last day of the Phase. Take the opportunity to talk about what the children have learned from reading and looking at persuasive texts and film trailers. Ask them to tell you the features of a persuasive text.	**HFWs:** because, good, but, so, not, does **Support:** children revisit key features of a persuasive text
	### Speaking and listening Talk about the trailers they have viewed. Show two trailers that the children have examined, perhaps including the one from the CD-ROM. Ask them to discuss the trailers and to evaluate and grade them. Which was the most successful at persuading the viewer to see the film? Why?	**Extend:** children give opinions supported by evidence
Reasoning: give reasons for opinions	### Independent work Ask the children to compare the two film trailers you have just discussed. Ask them to make notes about their opinions and to include evidence in support of them. Allow them 20 minutes to complete this activity.	
Communication: discuss ideas and communicate persuasively	### Plenary Choose two or three children to express their opinions to the class, using their notes to help them. Remind them to produce evidence from the sound and visual text to support their opinions. Encourage debate amongst the rest of the class. Note key findings from the children on the board for use in Phase 2.	**Support:** children use phonic skills to support note-writing

Guided reading
Provide the children with a 'persuasive text' book of your choice on animal habitats, climate change or other environmental issues. In group work, share the book together. Spend time discussing what they have read and then ask them to identify persuasive text features from the book. Encourage the children to use the key findings notes you made on the board at the end of Day 7 to check their findings against.

Assessment
Select a film trailer of your choice and one which the children have not already seen. Show the trailer and then ask them to evaluate how the soundtrack, voice-over, moving images and sound effects to persuade the viewer to see the film. Ask them to make notes to share with the others at the end of the session.
Invite each child to share their findings with the others. Check that each child has understood how to evaluate a trailer in this way.
Refer back to the learning outcomes on page 156.

Further work
Invite the children to visit the RSPB website. Invite the children to research climate change and its effect on bird populations. Tell them to make notes to support future writing on their findings. Provide further practice of examining how images provoke emotional responses using photocopiable page 164 'Emotional response'. Discuss the pictures with the children and the emotions they provoke. Ask the children to write explanations for their emotional responses.

DAY 1 ■ Planning promotional trailers

Key features	Stages	Additional opportunities
	### Introduction Prior to beginning this Phase, allow the children to watch the film *Watership Down* (copyright permitting). After enjoying the film together, encourage the children to discuss it in relation to science work you have been doing on habitats. Provide prompt questions to stimulate discussion, for example: *What impact can humans have on animals' habitats?*	**HFWs:** I, like, because, don't **MFWs:** think, thought **Support:** find correlations between topic work and fictional stories
	### Speaking and listening Tell the children that they are going to plan an imaginary promotional trailer for this film. Ask them to decide the purpose or impact they want their trailer to have. Ask the children what images, words and sounds would create the desired impact on the audience, for example the 'Bright Eyes' music sequence when Hazel hallucinates that he sees the Black Rabbit.	**Extend:** use elaborate vocabulary to express opinions
Communication: discuss ideas and communicate persuasively	### Independent work Ask the children to make brief notes on the key features of the film that carry the most impact for them and to give reasons for their choices. Allow them 15 minutes to complete this task.	
	### Plenary Invite children to share their work. Remind them to give reasons for their choices. Do the others agree with the choices made? How do they differ from their own?	

DAY 2 ■ Selecting key moments in a film

Key features	Stages	Additional opportunities
	### Introduction Remind the children of the work they did yesterday. Allow them to refer to the notes they made while reviewing this work.	**Support:** recall previous work
Information processing: use DVD controls to navigate and select key moments	### Speaking and listening Discuss key moments in the film, ones that could evoke an emotional response from the viewer. Would they be a good choice to include in a promotional trailer? Why? Use the scene selection option on the DVD main menu and the pause button on the control panel to locate one of the key moments. Model navigating through the DVD text. Demonstrate how to make notes on the suitability of clips (key moments). Encourage all the children to make suggestions.	**Extend:** use extended vocabulary to discuss sections of the film
Communication: discuss ideas and communicate persuasively	### Independent work Now invite the children to work in pairs to isolate another clip that they feel would evoke the type of response discussed earlier. Tell them to make notes about its suitability for inclusion in a promotional trailer, as demonstrated, with one child acting as scribe. Allow them 15 minutes to complete this task.	
Reasoning: give reasons for opinions	### Plenary Invite the children to decide the criteria by which they would judge the persuasiveness of the clips. Select two pairs of children to show their work and justify their choices. Encourage debate on the choices made. Do the others agree that the clips shown are the most evocative. Why/why not?	

DAY 3 ▪ Features that evoke emotional responses

Key features	Stages	Additional opportunities
	Introduction Talk about the work you have done so far on selecting clips (key moments) for a trailer for *Watership Down*. Can the children recall what the purpose or impact of the trailer was to be?	**Support:** revise earlier work
Communication: discuss ideas and communicate persuasively	**Speaking and listening** Talk about the way the film has been produced to evoke an emotional response from the viewer, for example the drab, muted colours of earthy brown and watery green in many scenes give a feeling of foreboding. Invite the children to think of other examples. Would examples such as these make good clips for a trailer? Ask a child to suggest particularly emotive clips that would be good to use in a trailer. Ask him or her to demonstrate how appropriate notes could be written about the clip. Encourage the others to make suggestions. However, remind them not to call out, but to wait their turn.	**Extend:** interrogate text to deepen understanding and response
Social skills: work collaboratively; listen to and respect others' ideas	**Independent work** Ask the children to repeat the process using copies of the same DVD (copyright permitting). Put the children into groups and ask them to record scenes on sticky notes using drawings and written notes. Allow them 20 minutes for this activity.	**Extend:** explore different ways of making notes
Reasoning: give reasons for opinions	**Plenary** When the time is up, bring the children back together. Choose spokespeople from the groups to explain their choices and give their reasons.	

DAY 4 ▪ Discussing and justifying choices

Key features	Stages	Additional opportunities
	Introduction Remind the children of the work they have completed to date. Choose a child to tell you the key features of a persuasive text. Ask the others to listen carefully and listen for errors. Where these occur, invite the others to suggest alternatives.	**Support:** revise key features of persuasive texts
Social skills: work collaboratively; listen to and respect others' ideas	**Speaking and listening** Ask the children to gather in the groups they worked in yesterday. Go round the groups asking them how their chosen clips will evoke the desired response from the viewer. Encourage each group to refer to their sticky notes. Remind them to listen while others speak and to wait patiently for their turn.	
Reasoning: give reasons for opinions **Evaluation:** review work using own assessment criteria	**Independent work** Remaining in their groups, ask the children to order their sticky notes in terms of each clip's effectiveness in provoking a desired response. Ask them to grade the clips from the most effective to the least. Ask them to justify their choices. Allow them 20 minutes to complete this task.	**Extend:** use extended vocabulary to explain reasons for choices
	Plenary At the end of the allotted time, bring the children back together. Select spokespeople from each group to show how they have graded their clips and their justifications for so doing according to criteria discussed in Day 2. Do the others agree with the choices made? How would they have graded the clips and why?	

DAY 5 ▪ Structuring and planning a trailer

Key features	Stages	Additional opportunities
	Introduction Review the progress made to date on selecting clips for the trailer. Ask the children to recall the response they want to evoke from the viewer. Do they think the clips selected will evoke such a response?	**Support:** revisit purpose of clips
Social skills: work collaboratively; listen to and respect others' ideas **Reasoning:** give reasons for opinions	**Speaking and listening** Demonstrate how to use the notes from Days 1 and 2 and the sticky notes from Days 3 and 4 to structure and plan a whole class trailer of *Watership Down*. Discuss how to build tension by ordering the clips so that they gradually give the viewer more information, for example Fiver's premonition when he sees the field red with blood; the images of the gas-filled warren and so on. Demonstrate how to order some of the scenes. Encourage the children to help you to make authorial choices about when to use the most effective clip for the greatest impact.	**Extend:** explore more adventurous vocabulary to justify authorial choices
Communication: discuss ideas and communicate persuasively	**Independent work** In their groups, ask the children to order the remaining scenes. Remind them to build up the suspense gradually. Encourage them to give reasons for their choices.	
	Plenary Invite children from each group to explain their choices. Have they built up the suspense to create the greatest impact?	

DAY 6 ▪ Discussing and giving opinions

Key features	Stages	Additional opportunities
	Introduction Discuss with the children of the main aim of the trailer they are planning as a class. Point out that *Watership Down* has been chosen because of its underlying message that humans can harm animals through not respecting their habitats. Point out that the aim of a trailer is to persuade people to see the film and also to give them an idea of what the film is about.	**Support:** revisit the theme of 'habitats' in science; practise organisational skills
Reasoning: give reasons for opinions	**Speaking and listening** Discuss the importance of organising the clips in such a way as to persuade the viewer to see the film. In particular, ask them to tell you which clips will have, in their opinion, the *greatest* effect on the viewer and why.	
Social skills: work collaboratively; listen to and respect others' ideas **Communication:** discuss ideas and communicate persuasively	**Independent work** In their groups, ask the children to organise their notes on the clips to persuade the viewer to see the film. Ask them also to plan their own trailer. Remind them to take turns to speak in the group and to listen while others are giving their opinions. Allow them 20 minutes for this task. If wished, a scribe in each group can make notes of decisions made to refer to during the plenary.	
	Plenary When the time is up, bring the class back together. Invite the children to tell you their plans on organising clips into trailers.	

DAY 7 ■ Checking plans against key features

Key features	Stages	Additional opportunities
	### Introduction Spend a few minutes reviewing the work done so far in this Phase. Select children to tell you the key features of a persuasive text. Ask them why a trailer is an important persuasive device. Elicit that a trailer only allows a few minutes to persuade a viewer to watch a whole film and must therefore evoke the right response in the intended audience.	**Support:** recall the purpose of a trailer as a persuasive device; use a checklist
Evaluation: review work using own assessment criteria	### Speaking and listening Using a child's plan from yesterday's task as an example demonstrate how to check it against the key features of the text type displayed on the board. Invite everyone to decide which key features have been used and which others might need to be addressed.	
Communication: discuss ideas and communicate persuasively	### Independent work Now ask the class to check their own plans in the same way. Encourage them to make notes about which features have been used and which might need to be addressed. Allow 15 minutes for this task.	
	### Plenary Ask two or three children to share their findings. How many key features had they used? How many needed to be addresses. Invite the whole class to discuss ways of addressing the missing features.	

Guided reading
Choose a trailer about wildlife and endangered habitats, either fictional or non-fictional. Invite the children to watch it as a group. Using the key features on the board ask them to identify those features which have been addressed and those which have not. Ask them to assess the effectiveness of the trailer in persuading the viewer to watch the film.

Assessment
Ask the children the key features of a persuasive text. Why is it important that trailers are persuasive? What should a trailer tell you? How can trailers evoke a response in people? What persuasive devices are used? Record the children's knowledge of persuasive texts and the use of persuasive devices in film trailers. Refer back to the learning outcomes on page 151.

Further work
Review several trailers for a wide variety of films. Ask the children to make notes about them and to rate their effectiveness as persuasive devices. Ask them to select one trailer that they feel is extremely persuasive and one which they feel could be improved upon. Ask them to make notes of their findings on photocopiable page 165 'Persuasive and non-persuasive trailers' of their findings to share with the others at the end of the session.

DAY 1 ◾ Increasing the persuasive nature of a trailer

Key features	Stages	Additional opportunities
	Introduction To introduce this last Phase, talk about the work the children have done so far on planning their own trailers. Ask them to recall the features of a persuasive text and how they used these as criteria when planning their own trailer for *Watership Down*. Tell the children that during this Phase they are going to write and present a final draft of their trailers.	**Support:** recall features of a persuasive text
Reasoning: give reasons for opinions **Social skills:** work collaboratively; listen to and respect others' ideas; take on roles within a group	**Speaking and listening** Discuss the elements of a trailer, for example voice-over, sound effects, music, images. Using a selection of the children's chosen key moments from the film, ask them to help you prepare a written draft or storyboard. Invite them to use the 'sticky note' method to identify where to increase the persuasive nature of the trailer. Which clips do the children think need a voice-over?	**Extend:** give reasons for choices unprompted
	Independent work In their groups, ask the children to examine their clips as you have demonstrated, to identify where to increase the persuasive nature of the trailer and where voice-overs would be most effective. Remind them to work collaboratively; taking turns to express their opinions.	
Evaluation: appraise each other's work	**Plenary** At the end of the session, bring the children back together. Ask a spokesperson from each group to share their work. Encourage peer appraisal.	

DAY 2 ◾ Writing voice-overs for trailers

Key features	Stages	Additional opportunities
	Introduction Remind the children of the work they did yesterday. Remind them of the importance of using voice-over, sound effects, music and images appropriately to trigger the required response in the viewer.	**HFWs:** and, but, so, because
	Speaking and listening Using key moments of your choice from *Watership Down*, model how to write a voice-over for a proposed trailer. Encourage the children to make suggestions. Take the opportunity to focus on the use of statements and questions as persuasive devices. Invite the children to suggest language that implies that *Watership Down* is a 'must see' film, using informal language and contractions to create an informal tone. Point out the need to use connectives to create a bridge across time lapses between their proposed clips in their storyboards.	**Extend:** use extended vocabulary to explain their ideas
Social skills: work collaboratively; listen to and respect others' ideas	**Independent work** In their groups, invite the children to write their own voice-over scripts to their storyboards, following the model done earlier. If wished, they may use photocopiable page 166 'Trailer information' to help them.	
Evaluation: review work using own assessment criteria	**Plenary** Refer to the language features of persuasive texts identified by the children earlier in this Unit. Invite them to evaluate their work under the different headings. Allow time for them to change their work as necessary.	

DAY 3 ■ Sound effects and music for trailers

Key features	Stages	Additional opportunities
	Introduction Review the work done to date on the proposed trailer. Point out that now the voice-overs are in place the children need to think about sound effects and music.	**HFWs:** first, last, now, then **MFWs:** sound **Support:** recall previous lessons in this Phase
Reasoning: give reasons for opinions	**Speaking and listening** Using the key moments you chose to demonstrate writing the voice-over, model how to decide where sound effects and music would add to the persuasive nature of the text. Point out that it is important to focus on the mood and pace rather than in identifying a specific track. A good example here might be the part where Fiver has a premonition when he imagines the warren filling with gas and being filled in. What sort of sound effects would add to this terrifying scene? Encourage the children to make suggestions and to justify them.	**Extend:** offer suggestions and justify their ideas
Social skills: work collaboratively; listen to and respect others' ideas; take on roles within a group	**Independent work** Now ask the children to work on their own drafts in their groups. Ask them to add notes to their plans to show where they think sound effects and music may be needed to add to the persuasive tone of the text. Allow the children 20 minutes to complete this task. Ask them to nominate a spokesperson to speak for the group during plenary.	
	Plenary At the end of the session, invite the spokesperson for each group to explain their choices. Ask the other children to offer suggestions or alternatives where appropriate.	

DAY 4 ■ Scanning visual images

Key features	Stages	Additional opportunities
	Introduction Ask the children to review their preparations so far on the proposed trailers for *Watership Down*. Point out that for the remaining three days of this Phase, they will be drafting the ICT text.	
Communication: drawing and scanning visual images; listening to instructions; asking questions	**Speaking and listening** Model how to draw and scan visual images from a storyboard into the computer. Insert the images into presentation software. Remind them to listen carefully to your instructions but to ask questions if they are unsure of any processes. Spend time after you have modelled this process to discuss with the children what you have done.	
Social skills: work collaboratively; listen to and respect others' ideas	**Independent work** Invite the children in their groups to draw and scan their own images from their storyboards into the computer. Remind them that this presentation is to be rough 'pitch' of an idea to a client and not a full trailer. Point out that because of this it does not have to be perfectly presented.	**Support:** support children when scanning their images
Evaluation: review work using own assessment criteria	**Plenary** At the end of the session, ask the children to assess the task. How many found it hard to achieve? How many coped well? Provide additional help for groups who found this task difficult. Invite all the groups to examine their drawn and scanned images to check that they are in the right order as per their storyboards.	

DAY 5 ▪ Adding voice-overs and sound effects

Key features	Stages	Additional opportunities
	Introduction Introduce today's work by pointing out that voice-overs and sound effects must now be added to the trailers of *Watership Down*.	**Extend:** use extended vocabulary to examine key scenes in film; give reasons for decisions
Social skills: work collaboratively; listen to and respect others' ideas	**Speaking and listening** Using the demonstration clips, model how to add voice-over and sound effects. Discuss the 'feel' of some of the scenes, for example when Hazel imagines he sees the Black Rabbit. Point out that dialogue may need to be recorded a few times, emphasising different words to create different effects on the audience.	
Communication: discuss ideas and communicate persuasively	**Independent work** In their groups ask the children to practise their voice-overs making notes where words need to be emphasised to create the required effect on the audience.	
	Plenary At the end of the session, ask spokespeople from the groups to explain the reasons for emphasising certain words in their scripts for the voice-overs.	

DAY 6 ▪ Presenting completed work

Key features	Stages	Additional opportunities
	Introduction Tell the children that they are going to add voice-overs and sound effects to their trailers.	**Extend:** act as mentors to suggest improvements in others' work
Social skills: work collaboratively; listen to and respect others' ideas	**Speaking and listening** Remind the children of the importance of an appropriate tone of voice in a voice-over, for example to reflect the seriousness of a clip. Invite two or three children to demonstrate this, with samples from their own scripts.	
Communication: discuss ideas and communicate persuasively	**Independent work** Ask the children to add their voice-overs and sound effects to their presentations. Remind them to refer to the plan and to imply that *Watership Down* is a 'must see' film.	**Support:** check criteria of persuasive texts
Evaluation: review work using own assessment criteria	**Plenary** Over two or three lessons, as needed, allow each group to show their presentations to the others. Do the trailers fit the criteria?	

Guided reading
Select other trailers of films that focus on animal habitats. Watch the trailers together. Ask the children to identify persuasive devices in the trailer, such as sound effects, voice-over, images. Ask them to identify a build-up of suspense to increase persuasive tone.

Assessment
Use the assessment activity 'Film trailers' from the CD-ROM to gauge the ability to analyse a film and identify effective scenes. Remind them to make notes as they watch the film. Check that the children have understood the key features of a persuasive text. Refer back to the learning outcomes on page 151.

Further work
Ask the children to choose a film trailer from a selection you give them. Ask them to compare this trailer with the one they created from a storyboard. Invite them to rate the sound effects, images, voice-overs in comparison with their own. Which trailer do they feel is more persuasive? Why?

Name ————————————————————— Date —————————

Advertisement

■ Read the advertisement. Underline and circle words, phrases and pictures that provoke emotion.

VOLUNTEERS NEEDED!

As many local people will know, our campaign to save our beautiful Martins Wood has failed. This last-remaining area of natural beauty in Maytown is to be destroyed next year to make way for a new housing development.

Now we need your help more than ever!

Can you help us save our birds?

Martins Wood Bird Support Group needs volunteers to build bird boxes to place in gardens bordering the Martins Wood area. We need to create safe alternative habitats to save our birds for the future of our environment.

If you can spare any time at all to help us- even for a few hours,
please telephone **01392 5073834**

Build a bird box...build a future for our birds! Their lives depend on it.

Image – Stock.xchng.

Name ———————————————————————— **Date** ————————————

Emotional response

■ Look at these pictures carefully. What emotions do they provoke? Do they provoke anger, pity or excitement? Write sentences to explain your choices.

————————————————————————
————————————————————————
————————————————————————
————————————————————————
————————————————————————
————————————————————————
————————————————————————
————————————————————————
————————————————————————
————————————————————————
————————————————————————
————————————————————————
————————————————————————
————————————————————————
————————————————————————
————————————————————————
————————————————————————
————————————————————————
————————————————————————
————————————————————————
————————————————————————
————————————————————————

PHOTOCOPIABLE ■SCHOLASTIC
www.scholastic.co.uk

Persuasive and non-persuasive trailers

■ Choose a persuasive and a non-persuasive trailer.

■ Write notes in the spaces below to justify your choices.

Persuasive trailer

Title of film: _____

What the film is about: _____

_____

_____

Details of the trailer: _____

_____

_____

The trailer is **persuasive** because: _____

_____

_____

Non-persuasive trailer

Title of film: _____

What the film is about: _____

_____

_____

Details of the trailer: _____

_____

_____

The trailer is **not persuasive** because: _____

_____

_____

Trailer information

■ Record the details of the clips you choose in each box. Write the voice-over script underneath. Add details of sound effects and music for each clip.

Clip identification: _____

_____

Voice-over: _____

_____

_____

_____

Sound effects: _____

_____

_____

Music: _____

_____

Clip identification: _____

_____

Voice-over: _____

_____

_____

_____

Sound effects: _____

_____

_____

Music: _____

_____

Clip identification: _____

_____

Voice-over: _____

_____

_____

_____

Sound effects: _____

_____

_____

Music: _____

_____

Clip identification: _____

_____

Voice-over: _____

_____

_____

_____

Sound effects: _____

_____

_____

Music: _____

_____

POETRY
UNIT 1 Creating images

Speak and listen for a range of purposes on paper and on screen

Strand 1 Speaking
- Respond appropriately to the contributions of others in light of differing viewpoints.

Read for a range of purposes on paper and on screen

Strand 6 Word structure and spelling
- Use knowledge of phonics, morphology and etymology to spell new and unfamiliar words.

Strand 7 Understanding and interpreting texts
- Explain how writers use figurative and expressive language to create images and atmosphere.

Strand 8 Engaging with and responding to texts
- Read extensively favourite authors or genres and experiment with other types of text.
- Interrogate texts to deepen and clarify understanding and response.
- Explore why and how writers write.

Write for a range of purposes on paper and on screen

Strand 9 Creating and shaping texts
- Develop and refine ideas in writing using planning and problem-solving strategies.
- Choose and combine words, images and other features for particular effects.

Strand 12 Presentation
- Write consistently with neat, legible and joined handwriting.

Progression in poetry

In this year children are moving towards:
- Describing a poem's impact and explaining own interpretation by referring to the poem.
- Commenting on the use of similes and expressive language to create images, sound effects and atmosphere.
- Discussing the poem's form and suggesting the effect on the reader.
- Varying volume and pace and using appropriate expression when performing.
- Using actions, sound effects, musical patterns and images to enhance a poem's meaning.
- Using language playfully to exaggerate or pretend; using similes to build images and identify clichés in own writing.
- Writing free verse; using repeating pattern; experimenting with simple forms.

Key aspects of learning covered in this Unit

Enquiry
Children will seek answers to their own and others' questions in reading.

Information processing
Children will explore and tease out ideas, thoughts and feelings communicated through the language and forms of poetry.

UNIT 1 ◄ **Creating images** *continued*

Evaluation
Children will share their own writing outcomes, as well as those of others. They will discuss success criteria, give feedback to others and judge the effectiveness of their own work.

Reasoning
Children will identify, explore and generate the mental connections represented by various forms of simple imagery – for example simile – a vital aspect of thinking, reasoning and understanding.

Empathy
In discussing and writing about the poems and their images, children will need to imagine themselves in another person's position.

Self-awareness
Children will discuss and reflect on their personal responses to the texts.

Communication
Children will develop their ability to discuss effective communication in respect of both the language and content of poetry they are reading and writing. They will sometimes work collaboratively in pairs and groups. They will communicate outcomes orally, and in writing (possibly including ICT).

Prior learning

Before starting this Unit check that the children can:
■ Describe the effect a poem has and suggest possible interpretations.
■ Discuss the choice of words and their impact, noticing how the poet creates 'sound effects' and 'pictures'.
■ Perform individually or chorally; vary volume, experimenting with expression, use pauses for effect and wordplay.
■ Use powerful nouns, adjectives and verbs, experimenting with alliteration.
■ Write simple free verse; borrow or create a repeating pattern.
If they need further support please refer to a prior Unit or a similar Unit in Year 3

Resources

Phase 1:
The Magic Box by Kit Wright ❦ ; *Last Night, I Saw the City Breathing* by Andrew Fusek Peters ❦; *A Snow and Ice poem* by Roger McGough ❦; *Being told off* by Fiona Tomlinson ❦; Musical instruments; Access to the internet; Selection of other poems; Photocopiable page 176 'List of similes'

Phase 2:
Last Night, I Saw the City Breathing by Andrew Fusek Peters ❦; *Being told off* by Fiona Tomlinson ❦; *Victoria Nicola Liked to Eat* by Trevor Millum ❦; Interactive activity 'Simile game' ❦; Photographs to stimulate simile-generation; Photocopiable page 176 'List of similes'; Photocopiable page 177 'Features of a poem'

Phase 3:
Using my senses by Fiona Tomlinson ❦; Instruments or objects for sound effects; Photocopiable page 177 'Features of a poem'; Photocopiable page 178 'Poem template'; Assessment activity 'Poem features' ❦

Cross-curricular opportunities

Music – use of percussion instruments

UNIT 1 ■ Teaching sequence

Phase	Children's objectives	Summary of activities	Learning outcomes
1	I can express how I feel about poems in appropriate language. I know what a simile is. I can identify how the language in poems is creating images.	Read poems from the CD-ROM and discuss children's responses. Focus on identifying the language that is creating 'pictures'/images in the poem. After reading a poem, make a list of sound effects and actions that help to highlight those images. Discuss the use of similes to create images in a poem. Perform their poems.	Children can recognise and discuss how poets use language (including similes and other simple images) to create a vivid picture in words. Children have increased the range of poetry of which they are aware and can discuss likes and dislikes, with reasons.
2	I can use similes to describe objects. I can use a poem to create a writing template. I can use a writing template to write a poem.	Read more poems and discuss responses. Use similes to describe specific objects. Read a poem and then use it to create a whole-class template. Write a template based on a poem read and use it to create own poem.	Children understand how to plan and write a poem based on a model.
3	I can identify features in a poem such as similes. I can use a poem to create a writing template use the template to write my own poem. I can perform my poem and then review it.	Examine features of poems. Use a poem to create a writing template and write own poems. Use similes and other words to create simple images. Children perform their poems to the rest of the class and then write a review about the features.	Children can write their own simple poem based on one previously read and analysed. Children can paint a vivid word picture using similes and other simple images.

Provide copies of the objectives for the children.

DAY 1 ■ Pictures in poems

Key features	Stages	Additional opportunities
Enquiry: describe a poem's impact	**Introduction** Display the three poems from the CD-ROM *Last Night, I Saw The City Breathing, The Magic Box* and *A Snow and Ice poem*. Read the first poem to the children and then ask them what they liked or disliked about it for example any familiar experiences, use of language, what 'pictures' are coming into their minds when they are reading the poem. Then read the other two and stop and ask children for their responses to them after each reading.	
Communication: working collaboratively in groups	**Speaking and listening** In groups of four, ask the children to choose one of the poems they have heard. After reading their poems aloud as a group, ask the children to discuss further any 'pictures' that they have after reading the poem again. Once they have read and discussed their poems, see if the children can think of any sound effects and actions to make it more dramatic/effective and to highlight those 'pictures' that the poem is creating.	**Support:** help to highlight the images that the poem creates **Extend:** find out what they think a simile is
Evaluation: discuss their work	**Plenary** Ask some of the groups to read the poem they have chosen and then say what sound effects and actions they would use. See if the groups would like to make any changes to their chosen sound effects and/or actions.	

DAY 2 ■ Similes

Key features	Stages	Additional opportunities
Enquiry and empathy: explore feelings communicated in poetry; describe the effects of a poem	**Introduction** Display the poem *Last Night, I Saw The City Breathing* from the CD-ROM. Read the poem and highlight any distinctive features of the poem such as the images, *Great gusts of people*. Ask the children what the poet is comparing the people to, for example wind, smoke from trains. Ask the children why they think the poet has chosen particular words/phrases, such as *cheek to cheek* in the line *Shadows were cheek to cheek with brick walls*. Remember to print out your annotated poem.	**Extend:** list any adjectives they think of
	Independent work Discuss what a simile is (comparing one thing to something of a different kind, used to make a description more vivid) and how poets use them to create images. Provide copies of the poem *Being told off* from the CD-ROM, ask the children to identify any similes in the poem. Encourage them to think about their own experiences of being told off.	**Support:** use photocopiable page 176 'List of similes' to help identify similes in the poem
	Plenary Ask some children to share any similes and any other features they have found and highlight these on the poems displayed. Print out the annotated poems.	

DAY 3 ■ Sounds

Key features	Stages	Additional opportunities
Communication: working collaboratively to understand the language and content of poetry	**Introduction** Read *Last Night, I Saw The City Breathing, The Magic Box* and *A Snow and Ice poem* from the CD-ROM. Ask the children to choose one of the poems and make a list the kinds of sound effects and actions they might use to illustrate key features. Ask the children how they might make those sounds, for example using their voices, using objects to create a sound. Introduce the musical instruments and/or sound effects from the CD-ROM as an option.	
Evaluation: give feedback to others; judge effectiveness of own work	**Speaking and listening** The children should be given time making the sounds and practicing them. Then stop them and ask them to take time to remember the actions they created in Day 1 that went with the poems. The children should practice these actions. Split the groups of four in two and ask one half to concentrate on the sound effects and the other half the actions. The children should now begin to 'perform' their poetry – rehearse their sound effects and actions.	**Extend:** make a mime sequence rather than a set of separate actions
	Plenary Ask each group to show their performance of their chosen poem to another group. Direct the watching group to respond to the performance by saying what they liked and did not like. Encourage the use of appropriate language.	**Support:** extend their thoughts by asking questions

DAY 4 ■ Performing a poem

Key features	Stages	Additional opportunities
Information processing: analyse a poem	**Introduction** Display *Last Night, I Saw The City Breathing* from the CD-ROM. Add the annotations (copy from the printed version in Day 2). Discuss with the children who performed this poem in Day 3 whether they captured all the images highlighted. You could also play the audio version from www.poetryarchive.org (copyright permitting) of the author reading the poem. Do the same for the other two poems.	**Extend:** visit poet's website www.tallpoet.com to find out more
Evaluation: assessing performances	**Speaking and listening** Let the children rehearse their performances from Day 3, making any changes as necessary. Ask each group to show their performances to the rest of the class. Tell the children watching they will be choosing a performance to review.	**Support:** extend children's reasons from just *like* and *dislike* to using more specific language
	Plenary Ask the children to choose one of the performances and review what they thought about it, for example how it recreated the images.	

Guided reading
Read *The Magic Box* and discuss the presentation of the poem and any punctuation. Ask the children questions such as: *Why did the poet skip a line of the repeating line* I will put in the box*?*

Assessment
Find different poems to give to the children in groups of four and ask them to read the poem and discuss its features. Listen to each group's responses to the poems. Ask the children to think of other similes. Refer to the learning outcomes from page 169.

Further work
Support: Read more poems and highlight with the children the images that are being created and discuss their own responses.
Extend: Write reviews on more poems.

DAY 1 ▪ Creating similes

Key features	Stages	Additional opportunities
	### Introduction Display *Last Night, I Saw The City Breathing* from the CD-ROM. Add the annotations (copy from the printed version from Phase 1). Refresh the children's memories by reading the poem aloud and then look at the features. Use photocopiable page 177 'Features of a poem' as an aide-memoire.	
Information processing: comment on similes and create images; use language playfully	### Speaking and listening Play a simile game. Divide the class into two groups and ask one group to think of random nouns, such as *tree, banana,* and the other group to think of adjectives, such as to describe speed: *fast, slow.* Ask for an adjective and then add one of the nouns adding *as a* in the middle. See how many similes they can make.	**Support:** complete the interactive activity 'Simile game' from the CD-ROM
	### Independent work Divide the class into three groups . Give one of the groups random objects; tell another to use the sound effects from the CD-ROM; and the last group to use photographs of your choice. Ask the children to work independently and to think and write down similes in response to their given items.	
	### Plenary Read *Being told off* from the CD-ROM identify the similes *as cold as ice, as black as thunder* and *as quiet as a mouse.* Explain that these are clichés meaning they are overused similes and therefore are not original and interesting. Can the children think of any others? For example, *cool as a cucumber.*	**Support:** give the children a list of adjectives to choose from

DAY 2 ▪ Class poem

Key features	Stages	Additional opportunities
Self-awareness: discuss poem's form and the effect on the reader. Information processing and empathy	### Introduction Display the poem *Victoria Nicola Liked to Eat* from the CD-ROM. Read it to the children. Discuss with the children their likes and dislikes about the poem and any features that they notice, for example the repetition of the first and second lines, the rhyming of the descriptive words in the last line. As the children discuss the features, annotate the poem.	
	### Shared work Tell the children you are going to write a poem using *Victoria Nicola Liked to Eat* as a model. Write a 'template' using the features of the poem: the repeated lines and so on. Think about a character who does something to excess and then something happens to them, a character who plays games competitively and so on. Remember to repeat the 'excesses' as in *Victoria Nicola Liked to Eat.* Once you have completed the template use it to write a poem based on the features of *Victoria Nicola Liked to Eat.*	**Support:** Highlight rhyming words and their spellings; discuss what is making the 'rhyme' **Extend:** highlight half rhymes
Communication: perform poetry	### Plenary Read the poem aloud. Think of any sound effects that the poem could have. Choose some children to 'perform' these sound effects when you read the poem again.	

DAY 3 ◢ My poem

Key features	Stages	Additional opportunities
Evaluation and self-awareness: assessing and improving own work	**Introduction** Re-read the poem that was written in Day 2, focusing on similes and imagery. Ask the children if they can think of any changes they would make to create better images. You might want to depart from the exact model of the poem: instead of having rhyming adjectives in the last line perhaps think of similes. Compare the features of the poem with other annotated poems that have been read.	**Support:** provide photocopiable page 177 'Features of a poem' **Spelling:** focus on homophones
Communication: use similes to build images; write with a repeating pattern	**Independent work** In pairs, ask the children to write their own poems based on the template. Tell the children to use template from Day 2. Remind the children they need a name that rhymes. **Plenary** Read some of the poems aloud or ask children to volunteer to read their own poems. Highlight any interesting phrases or ideas the children have written. Ask them why they have chosen particular words and so on.	

Guided reading

Read the poem *Victoria Nicola Liked to Eat* and focus on the presentation on the poem and how the repetition and the rhyme help to make the humour. See if the children can highlight any commas and apostrophes.

Assessment

In pairs, ask children to read their poems to one another and write down a list of their own features or annotate a copy of their poem.
Refer to the learning outcomes on page 169.

Further work

Support: Use the simile list on photocopiable page 176 and ask the children if they understand what images each simile is evoking. Ask the children if they can think of others they might know.
Extend: Ask the children to find out what the word *metaphor* means. See if they can express the differences between a metaphor and a simile.

DAY 1 ■ Poem templates

Key features	Stages	Additional opportunities
Enquiry and self-awareness: respond to a poem	### Introduction Display the poem *Using my senses* from the CD-ROM and ask the children for their response to the poem. ### Speaking and listening Guide the children in using more appropriate language when they are describing their likes and dislikes. Display the poem and highlight any features that the children have mentioned. Ask the children to compare the poem with the other poems that they have read, for example compare the layout, subject and language.	
Communication: write free verse; experiment with simple forms	### Independent work Tell the children they are going to write a poem using the poem *Using my senses* as a model. In pairs, let children develop their own template of the poem. Ask the children to decide what form they want to use for the poem as their template, for example two lines in each verse, starting each verse *I like...* and decide on their subject. Ask some of the pairs to explain their templates to the rest of the group. ### Plenary Encourage all the children to think of any sound effects for their poems. Ask them to make a list.	**Support:** use photocopiable page 178 'Poem template'

DAY 2 ■ Writing poems

Key features	Stages	Additional opportunities
	### Introduction Display the poem *Using my senses* from the CD-ROM. Re-read the poem and ask the children to compare their templates with the poem. Revisit the features of the poem from Day 1.	
Communication: write free verse; experiment with simple forms	### Independent work The children use their templates they made in their pairs to then write their own poems independently. When they have finished writing their poems ask the children to remember the sound effects they thought of in Day 1. Use a variety of objects to create the sound effects. ### Plenary Once they have finished ask them to read their poems aloud to their partner with their sound effects. Ask the children to discuss the differences between theirs and their partner's poems. Encourage the children to make any changes they need in order to create strong images for the reader.	**Extend:** use sound effects from the internet (copyright permitting)

DAY 3 ■ Performing poems

Key features	Stages	Additional opportunities
Enquiry: examine imagery	### Introduction Remind the children about the features of poems from photocopiable page 177 or the list made from the annotated poems from previous Phases. Focus on how the poets create imagery and how the reader of the poem can help to emphasise this. Choose a poem (either from one in previous phases or one you know well.) Read the poem with little expression first and then read it with expression. Discuss with the children which was the better reading.	
Evaluation: appraise performances	### Speaking and listening Encourage any volunteers to perform their poems to the rest of the class. Ask the rest of the class to make notes on the performances.	**Spelling focus:** homophones
	### Independent work Ask the children to write their own review of the process of creating and performing their poem as well as reviewing some of the performances they have seen.	**Support:** work as a group and teacher acts as a scribe
	### Plenary Ask some children to share their reviews with the rest of the class.	

Guided reading
Read a chosen poem and ask the children to identify any images that are being created and any similes that the poet uses. Draw attention to the punctuation of the poem. Ask the children if it is different from the punctuation in a story, perhaps capital letters starting every line.

Assessment
Work through the assessment on the CD-ROM – Identifying features of poems.
Refer to the learning outcomes from page 169.

Further work
Support: Read some rhyming poems and ask the children to identify the rhyme. Discuss where the rhyme is, for example at the end of each line, every other line... Extend: Choose a poet and conduct research about the poet by using books and the internet. Find out any other poems that they have written.

List of similes

Cool as a cucumber.

Black as thunder.

Brave as a lion.

As bright as a button.

2+2=4

Shaking like a leaf.

As dry as a bone.

As quiet as a mouse.

As hard as nails.

100 LITERACY FRAMEWORK LESSONS YEAR 4

PHOTOCOPIABLE ■SCHOLASTIC
www.scholastic.co.uk

Features of a poem

Theme

What is the poem about? An animal? A person? A feeling?

Feelings

What does the poem make you feel, for example happy, sad?

Alliteration

Does the poet use words with the same first letter?

For example: *The mad monkey moodily ate the mango.*

Nouns/adjectives/verbs

What sorts of powerful words does the poet use?

For example: *The crashing storm of children flooded the playground.*

Expressive language and similes

Can you spot any similes? What images are being created?

Rhyme

Does the poem rhyme?

For example: *There sat the watching cat, it sat and watched the rat.*

Rhythm

How does the poem sound when you read it. Is it slow or fast?

Patterns

Does the poem have any repeating lines?

For example: *I like my friend, I like my books, I like…*

Form

How is the poem written? For example, does the poem have rhyming couplets? Is it a haiku? Is it free verse?

Poem template

POETRY ■ UNIT 1

I like smelling

_____

_____

I like watching

_____

_____

I like walking

_____

_____

I like touching

_____

_____

I like seeing

_____

_____

I like listening

_____

_____

100 LITERACY FRAMEWORK LESSONS YEAR 4

Illustrations © Peter Lubach/Beehive Illustration.

POETRY
UNIT 2 Exploring form

Speak and listen for a range of purposes on paper and on screen

Strand 1 Speaking
- Respond appropriately to the contributions of others in the light of differing viewpoints.

Read for a range of purposes on paper and on screen

Strand 7 Understanding and interpreting texts
- Explain how writers use figurative and expressive language to create images and atmosphere.

Strand 8 Engaging with and responding to texts
- Read extensively favourite authors or genres and experiment with other types of text.
- Interrogate texts to deepen and clarify understanding and response.
- Explore why and how writers write, including through face-to-face and online contact with authors.

Write for a range of purposes on paper and on screen

Strand 9 Creating and shaping texts
- Choose and combine words, images and other features for particular effects.

Strand 12 Presentation
- Write consistently with neat, legible and joined handwriting.
- Use word-processing packages to present written work and continue to increase speed and accuracy in typing.

Progression in poetry

In this year children are moving towards:
- Describing a poem's impact and explaining their own interpretation by referring to the poem.
- Commenting on the use of similes and expressive language to create images, sound effects and atmosphere.
- Discuss the poem's form and suggesting the effect on the reader.
- Varying volume and pace and using appropriate expression when performing; using actions, sound effects, musical patterns and images to enhance a poem's meaning.
- Using language playfully to exaggerate or pretend; using similes to build images and identify clichés in own writing.
- Writing free verse; using a repeating pattern; experimenting with simple forms.

▶

UNIT 2 ◀ Exploring form *continued*

Key aspects of learning covered in this Unit

Self-awareness
Children will discuss and reflect on their personal responses to the texts.

Reasoning
Children will explain their opinions about different poems and use particular words and phrases to support or illustrate their ideas.

Creative thinking
Children will have the opportunity to respond imaginatively to the stimulus of a first-hand experience and may be able to express their response by presenting poetry through sound and image to enhance its meaning.

Evaluation
Children will have regular opportunities to review their work against agreed success criteria. They will view their own and their peers' presentations and discuss ways to improve them.

Social skills
When designing group presentations, children will learn about relating to the other group members effectively.

Communication
Children will often work collaboratively in pairs and groups. They will communicate outcomes orally, in writing and through ICT.

Prior learning

Before starting this Unit check that the children can:
■ Describe the effect a poem has and suggest possible interpretations.
■ Discuss the choice of words and their impact, noticing how the poet creates 'sound effects' by using alliteration, rhythm or rhyme and creates 'pictures' using similes.
■ Use actions, voices, sound effects and simple musical patterns to add to a performance.
If they need further support please refer to a prior Unit or a similar Unit in Year 3.

Resources

Phase 1:
Snowflakes fall softly by Fiona Tomlinson ❧; *The Romans in Britain* by Judith Nicholls ❧; Access to the internet; Selection of poetry anthologies; Objects, instruments and ICT tools to create sound effects; Photocopiable page 190 'Sound effects'; Photocopiable page 191 'Poem review sheet'
Phase 2:
Woodland and lake photographs ❧; Image-editing software; Sound effects and voice recorders; *Being told off* by Fiona Tomlinson ❧; *Snowflakes fall softly* by Fiona Tomlinson ❧; *Using my senses* by Fiona Tomlinson ❧; Digital cameras; Photocopiable page 192 'Poem map'; Interactive activity 'The Romans are here' ❧
Phase 3:
Selection of poems for reading aloud; children's presentations and relevant software from Phase 2; Assessment activity 'Poems' ❧

Cross-curricular opportunities

ICT – using digital cameras, graphics package, recording software (hardware), presentation software
Geography – weather
History – Romans

UNIT 2 ■ Teaching sequence

Phase	Children's objectives	Summary of activities	Learning outcomes
1	I can discuss a poem using appropriate language. I understand the use of descriptive language in a poem. I know how to identify different features in a poem. I can read a poem out loud with expression.	Read a haiku poem and discuss its features. Highlight features of the poem. Read a poem and compare reading to oneself and reading aloud. Make a list of the features of the poem. Annotate a poem and discuss the features. Think of sound effects for the poem. Record the poem using sound effects.	Children listen for and use some technical terms in discussion of poems. Children understand how the use of expressive and descriptive language can create effects or generate emotional responses. Children can experiment orally with phrases and words to create different effects and responses.
2	I know how to change digital photographs. I can work in a group collaboratively. I can present and evaluate my own poem.	Look at how to manipulate photographs. Choose poems to illustrate with photographs. Take photographs to illustrate a poem and manipulate the pictures to create effects. Assign speaking roles for children to read and record the poem. Find sound effects for their poem and add these to the photographs in presentation software. Present poem to another group.	Children can plan, organise and create an ICT-based poetry presentation that involves each member of the group. Children can present and perform a poem.
3	I can evaluate other group's poems and express myself appropriately.	Evaluate poem from audience response and make any changes. Present poem to wider audience.	Children can reflect on and evaluate the quality of their own and their peers' poetry presentations.

Provide copies of the objectives for the children.

DAY 1 ■ Haikus

Key features	Stages	Additional opportunities
Self-awareness: reasoning, explaining opinions	**Introduction**	
	Display the haiku poem *Snowflakes fall softly* from the CD-ROM. Ask the children to read the poem to themselves. Once they have read the poem, ask them to say what they liked and disliked about it and give reasons. Encourage them to think about the use of language, imagery and so on. Make a list of the children's responses to the poem.	
Communication: work collaboratively	Explain the haiku form and where the form originates. (A Japanese poem of 17 syllables, in three lines of five, seven and five. They traditionally evoke the natural world.)	
	Speaking and listening	**Support:** as a group, read the poem aloud and discuss difference; use the list written in introduction
	Ask the children to read the poem aloud to a partner. See if the children notice a difference between reading the poem to themselves and hearing it read aloud, for instance emphasis different on words.	
	Independent work	
	Provide the children with a copy of the poem and ask them to highlight features such as language used, images created.	**Extend:** Can they find out what a cinquin is?
	Plenary	
	Look at the poem on display and note down all the children's further observations on the poem.	

DAY 2 ■ Reading poems aloud

Key features	Stages	Additional opportunities
Self-awareness: personal responses, explain opinions, describe images, comment on language used	**Introduction**	
	Display the poem *The Romans in Britain* from the CD-ROM and ask the children to read the poem to themselves.	
	Now read the poem to the children or go to the website www.poetryarchive.org and hear the poet reading the poem. Ask the children to tell you if there are any differences between when they read the poem and when the poem was read aloud, for example ask them if the poet highlighted/ emphasised anything different from when the children read the poem to themselves.	
Communication: work collaboratively	**Speaking and listening/Independent work**	**Extend:** find out information on the poet
	Divide the class into groups of four and provide a variety of poetry books for the children to read. Ask them to choose a couple of poems that they think would be good to read aloud. Give the children a time limit so that they do not take too long in choosing. The children should practise reading the poems in their groups.	**Support:** as a group read the poems and make a list of features
	Ask them to make a list of the features of the poems such as any repetition, rhyme, similes and other use of language that they think is effective in creating images. Use the list from Day 1 as a reference.	
	Plenary	
	Choose some groups to read their poems aloud. Add more features to the list made on Day 1 that the children have found in the poems they have looked at.	

DAY 3 ■ Sounds for poems

Key features	Stages	Additional opportunities
Self-awareness: note similes and expressive language, effects on the reader, personal responses **Communication:** work collaboratively in performance	**Introduction** Re-read the poem written in Unit 1, Phase 2, Days 2/3. If you can, display it on the whiteboard. Ask the children to remember the features of the poem and anything they liked and disliked. Annotate the poem using the whiteboard tools. Use the list from Day 1 to add any other features that might be relevant. **Speaking and listening** In groups of four, ask the children to read the poem aloud using photocopiable page 190 'Sound effects' to write down any words or images which give them ideas for sound effects. Tell the children to make a list of what they use to create the sound effects. Highlight that they are not constrained to using just actual instruments and that most objects can make a sound. **Plenary** Ask the children to share some of their ideas for sound effects. Choose which ones you think would be effective and easy to create and write them up as a list.	**Support:** act as a scribe for the children **Extend:** children could be encouraged to find sound effects from internet sites

DAY 4 ■ Presenting poems

Key features	Stages	Additional opportunities
Communication: perform poetry **Evaluation:** review own poems	**Introduction** Display the poem written in Unit 1, Phase 2, Day 2/3 on the whiteboard. Perhaps ask some children to read a verse each. **Speaking and listening** In groups of four, ask the children to choose some sound effects either from the class list in the plenary from Day 3 or from their own lists. Discuss in their groups how they might perform the poem, for example, will they all read it, read a verse each... Then record the poem on the computer and record any sound effects. Children can use the sound effects from the CD-ROM or any that they create themselves. **Independent work** Ask the children to write up their poems from Unit 1 as if they are going to be part of an anthology. Look at some poetry books, especially ones with pictures. Ask the children to examine how the poems are being presented, for example any illustrations, the layout of the poem. Ask the children to draw pictures to illustrate their poems. **Plenary** Encourage children to listen to and review their poems using photocopiable page 191 'Poem review sheet'.	**Support:** help children to work collaboratively **Support:** some children might find it easier to use the computer to write a group poem

UNIT 2 ☐ PHASE 1

Guided reading

Read the poem *The Romans in Britain* and ask the children why the poet chose the particular Roman inventions she writes about, such as aqueducts.

See if the children can find another poem by the same poet.

Assessment

Listen to and review another group's poem using appropriate language.

Ask the children questions about their own poems and see if they can use appropriate language.

Refer to the learning outcomes from page 186.

Further work

Support: Provide a list of words and phrases that help to describe the various features of a poem so that they can use this when reviewing poems.

Extend: Find other poems from the poets studied. Write a short biography.

DAY 1 ■ Images in poetry

Key features	Stages	Additional opportunities
Self-awareness: discuss personal responses and explain opinions	**Introduction** Display the woodland and lake photographs from the CD-ROM. Ask the children what the photographs show, and encourage other responses to them. Copy and paste the photograph into a graphics program. (If you do not have a program already on your computer you can download free software from picasa.google.com.) Demonstrate how you can manipulate a photograph to create different effects by changing the colour, using a soft focus and so on. While you create the effects save each photograph and then display them on the whiteboard. Compare the different effects for example is there now more of a focus on one object in the photograph, how does changing the colour of the photograph change the image?	**ICT:** use a graphics program **Support:** some children might need more time to understand how to use the software
Communication: working collaboratively	**Independent work** In groups of six ask the children to choose a poem either *Being told off, Using my senses, Snowflakes fall softly* or other poems they have written themselves. Once they have chosen a poem, ask the children to read it aloud in their group and note down any photographs they could take to illustrate the poem. Tell the children that they are going to illustrate the poems with pictures that they take around the school. Ask if they have chosen the best poem for that.	
Evaluation: self-assess	**Plenary** Let children review their choices and make changes if necessary.	

DAY 2 ■ Photographing poetry

Key features	Stages	Additional opportunities
Communication and self-awareness: express and explain reasons	**Introduction** Before the lesson, you might want to ask for extra digital cameras for the groups to use. You may also need extra adults to help the children use the cameras and to upload the images onto the computer. Briefly demonstrate again how to manipulate photographs to create different effects as a reminder to the children. Make a list of rules about how the children should take photographs around the school, including where can they can go, how not to disturb other classes.	**ICT focus:** using a digital camera
	Speaking and listening The children use the list they made in Day 1 and take the photographs they have planned using a digital camera. Make sure that they have also made a plan as to who will take which photograph: will it be one person or will they share?	**Support:** devise the plan with the group
	Independent work Once they have taken their photographs and uploaded onto the computer, let children use graphics software to manipulate the images to create effects that illustrate the poem. Ask the children to make a list of what they do to each photograph so that they can record the process.	**Support:** help with reviewing the photographs, perhaps with a template/form
Evaluation: self-assess	**Plenary** Ask the children to review some of the photographs and effects they have created and note down any changes they would like to make.	

DAY 3 ■ Presenting poetry

Key features	Stages	Additional opportunities
	Introduction	**ICT:** cutting and pasting skills; using presentation software
	Explain to the children that they are going to create a presentation of their poems using the photographs that they took yesterday. In their groups of six, they will be recording the poems and adding sound effects and will present their poems to the rest of the class and then to another class or to the whole school.	
Communication: work collaboratively in performance	Using a digital picture, demonstrate how to cut and paste their pictures into a presentation software package.	
	Tell the children that they are going to need to assign speaking roles for the poem, for example are they going to read a verse each or if there is any dialogue is one person going to 'be the character'? Ask the children to decide on who will be speaking and what they will be doing. Perhaps split the group so that two are concentrating on speaking the poem and the other two are sourcing any sound effects they might want to use with their poem while the other two are putting the photographs into the presentation software.	
Creative thinking: combine text and images	**Independent work**	**Support:** help with using the template
	(You might need extra adult support to help the children use the software.) Plan how the photographs and the audio of the poem and any sound effects will fit together. Use a storyboard template, such as an enlarged copy of photocopiable page 192 'Story map' to map out which photographs and audio files go with which part of the poem. It might help to write out the poem. Record the poem and create the appropriate files to be used in the presentation software. Add the audio to the photographs.	
Evaluation: decide success criteria	**Plenary**	
	Discuss and make a list of success criteria for the poem, for example, how well do the pictures illustrate the poem? Does the audio help to highlight any similes?	

DAY 4 ■ Presenting poetry

Key features	Stages	Additional opportunities
	Introduction	
	The children will probably need this day to complete Day 3 activities. Tell the children that they will now present their poems to another group. Arrange which group will present to which group.	
Communication: perform poems	**Speaking and listening**	**Support:** help children to understand the success criteria
	Invite each group to show the presentation to another group and then ask the audience group what they liked and disliked. Use the success criteria list from Day 3. Make sure that the children are not just concentrating on the visual but also the audio, the sound effects and how the poem was being read.	
Evaluation: appraise peers' work	**Plenary**	
	Ask the groups to make any changes that they want to in response to the audience's reactions	

Guided reading

Read the poem the children have chosen and note down any similes, words or phrases that create images.
See if they can identify any homophones and discuss the differences.

Assessment

Ask the children to write a review of their poem and the process that it took to create the presentation.
Refer to the learning outcomes from page 181.

Further work

Support: As a group exercise look at the interactive activity on the CD-ROM *The Romans are Here* and fill in the two blank lines using the suggestions under the poem. Discuss the poem and the additional lines.
Extend: Ask the children to find out about a chosen poet. If possible, write an email or letter to a poet about what they like about the poet's work.

DAY 1 ■ Evaluating poetry

Key features	Stages	Additional opportunities
Self-awareness: describe and explain a poem and comment on figurative language using appropriate vocabulary **Evaluation:** explain opinions	**Introduction** Read a poem of your choice to the children. Ask them what they thought of your reading: was the pace right; did you read with expression? Did the reading of the poem create vivid images? Write the children's responses down and add to the features list begun at the beginning of the Unit. **Speaking and listening** Display the list above. Say that these are features of how poems are written and spoken and that they will use these features to 'judge' their presentations of their poems. **Independent work** Each group shows their presentations from Phase 2, Day 4 to the rest of the class. After each presentation ask what the children liked/disliked about the presentations and refer to the feature lists. **Plenary** Encourage each child to evaluate the presentations, for example how well they thought the photographs, audio and so on presented the poem.	**Support:** guide children in using appropriate language; word cards with 'features' on might be useful prompts **Extend:** write a review

DAY 2 ■ Presenting poems to a wider audience

Key features	Stages	Additional opportunities
Evaluation: adapt work in light of reviews **Communication:** perform poetry	**Introduction** As a whole class remind the children of their reviews and ask them if they need to make any changes to their poems either from comments made by other children or from Phase 1, Day 3. **Independent work** Make time for the children to make any changes to their poems. Show their poems to another audience – either to another class or in assembly. If possible, publish their poems on the school's website. **Plenary** If you need time to finish off their evaluations of the project then give the children some time to reflect on the whole process from selecting the poem to showing it to other audiences.	

Guided reading

Choose a selection of poems. Ask the children to read them. Discuss the language and any 'hard' words. Ask the children how they 'tackled' these words and see if they were able to work out the meaning of the word.

Assessment

Use the end of Unit assessment on the CD-ROM – self-assessment about what the children know about features of poems.

Refer to the learning outcomes from page 181.

Further work

Support: Read a couple of poems you have chosen. Ask the children what they like/dislike about the poems. Guide them in using appropriate language.

Extend: Using a selection of poems classify the type, for example haiku, rhyming, free verse.

POETRY

UNIT 2 ☐ PHASE 3

Sound effects

Words or phrases from poem	Sound effects

Poem review sheet

◼ Use this sheet to review your poem. Fill in the boxes below.

What you liked/disliked?	Are there any similes?

Write down any interesting words or expressive language.	What sound effects were used?

Any extra features:

Poem map

Line/verse: Audio: Sound effects: Photograph:	Line/verse: Audio: Sound effects: Photograph:
Line/verse: Audio: Sound effects: Photograph:	Line/verse: Audio: Sound effects: Photograph:
Line/verse: Audio: Sound effects: Photograph:	Line/verse: Audio: Sound effects: Photograph:

100 LITERACY FRAMEWORK LESSONS YEAR 4